STUDIES IN NORTH-EASTERN HISTORY

The Battle of Neville's Cross

1346

STUDIES IN NORTH-EASTERN HISTORY

Series editor: Professor A. J. Pollard

1. *Symeon of Durham. Historian of Durham and the North*, ed. David Rollason (1998)

2. *The Battle of Neville's Cross 1346*, ed. David Rollason and Michael Prestwich (1998)

3. *Late Medieval Northallerton. A Small Market Town and its Hinterland, c.1470–1540*, by Christine M. Newman (forthcoming)

Studies in North-Eastern History is a series published by Shaun Tyas for the North-East England History Institute, which is based on a confederation of the six north-east universities (Durham, Newcastle, Northumbria, Open University, Sunderland and Teesside), has links with local bodies and individuals in tourism, heritage, museums, libraries, historical and other groups in the community, and fosters research at the highest level through conferences, research groups and research projects on all aspects of North-East England's past.

STUDIES IN NORTH-EASTERN HISTORY

THE BATTLE

of

NEVILLE'S CROSS

1346

Edited by

David Rollason

and

Michael Prestwich

SHAUN TYAS

STAMFORD

1 9 9 8

Typeset from the disc of the editors and published by

SHAUN TYAS
(an imprint of Paul Watkins)
for the North-East England History Institute
18 Adelaide Street
Stamford
Lincolnshire
PE9 2EN

ISBN
1 900289 19 9 (hardback)
1 900289 20 2 (paperback)

Printed and bound by Woolnoughs of Irthlingborough

CONTENTS

PREFACE

The 650th anniversary of the Battle of Neville's Cross was celebrated on the very site where the conflict took place, with a conference and, on the following day, a spirited, if damp, reconstruction of the fighting. This volume contains most of the papers given at the conference. The circumstances that led to the battle, and the course of the fighting, are discussed in two papers, Michael Prestwich taking an English point of view, and Alexander Grant a Scottish. This does not result from any notable chauvinism on the part of the two authors, but viewing the battle from a different perspective, and with an emphasis on different sources, helps to demonstrate some of the difficulties involved in analysing a complex event. Two of the leading participants on the English side are the subject of detailed studies; Marie Dixon examines the ill-fated career of John de Coupland, captor of the Scottish king David II, while Robin Frame's study unravels the career of Thomas Rokeby, sheriff of Yorkshire, one of the English commanders. The fate of the Black Rood of Scotland and the tradition that it was captured from the Scots at the battle is then explained by Lynda Rollason. The structure of the estates of Durham Cathedral Priory played a significant part in determining the course of the campaign. This, with the topography, is examined by Richard Lomas. The cross itself no longer survives in any substantial form, though a stump overlooks the busy crossroads that is Neville's Cross today. It had, however, a notable history, which is elucidated by Linda Drury, and this volume also publishes a new reconstruction of the cross by Martin Roberts, together with a note on the geology of the present remains by G. A. L. Johnson. Robert Hardy then sets the battle in the context of the development of military archery.

An appendix provides translations by Mark Arvanigian and Antony Leopold of the letters and main chronicle accounts of the battle, together with extracts from the account roll detailing payments to the English troops. Detailed cross-references to these documents are not given in the various papers, although attention is drawn to them in the first reference in each paper; we hope that this will not cause readers any difficulty. We are very grateful to Professor D. E. R. Watt and the University of St Andrews for allowing us to include the translation of the account of the battle from the *Scotichronicon*.

We are grateful to Yvonne Beadnell for drawing the maps; we make no excuse for not providing a diagram of the traditional type setting out the disposition of the troops on the battlefield, for the sources simply do not permit any accurate reconstruction to be made.

Financial assistance in the work of translation has been provided by Durham County Council, which we acknowledge with gratitude. We are also grateful to Lesley Hehir and David Butler of Durham County Council, to Martin Roberts of Durham City Council, to Mr Barry Owens and the staff of the Durham Johnston Comprehensive School, and to Miss Tracy Swaddle of the University of Durham History Department for their invaluable assistance in a myriad of ways in making the conference the success that it was.

The conference was the first major event to be sponsored by the North-East England History Institute.

David Rollason
Michael Prestwich
University of Durham
May 1997

LIST OF ILLUSTRATIONS

ABBREVIATIONS

ASC	Durham University Library, Archives and Special Collections
CCR	*Calendar of the Close Rolls preserved in the Public Record Office: Edward III* (14 vols., London, 1896–1913)
CDS	*Calendar of Documents Relating to Scotland*, i–iv, ed. J. Bain (Edinburgh, 1881–6), v, ed. J. Galbraith (Edinburgh, 1986)
CPR	*Calendar of the Patent Rolls preserved in the Public Record Office: Edward III* (16 vols., London, 1891–1916)
DCDCM	Durham Cathedral, Dean and Chapter Muniments
Jean le Bel	*Chronique de Jean le Bel*, ed. J. Viard and E. Déprez (2 vols., Paris, 1904–5)
Lanercost	*Chronicon de Lanercost*, ed. J. Stevenson (Maitland Club, Edinburgh, 1839)
NCH	*A History of Northumberland, issued under the direction of the Northumberland County History Committee* (15 vols., Newcastle upon Tyne and London, 1893–1940)
RS	Rolls Series
Rot. Scot.	*Rotuli Scotiae in Turri Londinensi et in domo capitulari Westmonasterii asservati*, ed. D. Macpherson *et al* (2 vols., London, 1814–19)
Surtees	R. Surtees, *The History and Antiquities of the County Palatine of Durham* (4 vols., Durham, 1816–40)
SS	Surtees Society
VCH Durham	*The Victoria County History of Durham*, ed. W. Page (London, 1905–)

The English at the Battle of Neville's Cross

MICHAEL PRESTWICH

Turning points in history are not always easy to recognise, but the Battle of Neville's Cross was a decisive moment in the long conflict between England and Scotland in the later middle ages. It was one of a series of remarkable English victories in the years 1346-7. The most celebrated is perhaps the Battle of Crécy. The first significant engagement of the period, however, took place in Brittany, where Sir Thomas Dagworth was surprised by a much larger force under Charles of Blois at Saint-Pol de Leon on 9 June. Crécy, fought in Ponthieu, followed on 26 August. On 17 October 1346 the Scots were defeated at Neville's Cross. The capture of Charles of Blois in Brittany, achieved as a result of a high-speed night march by Sir Thomas Dagworth, at La Roche-Derrien, on 20 June 1347 was yet another triumph. That was followed up by the surrender of Calais, eventually achieved on 3 August 1347 after an eleven-month siege. Each of these triumphs was surprising, and explanation of English success is not easy. Of them all, the victory at Neville's Cross is perhaps the least simple to account for in military terms.

The context of all the victories was that of the great Anglo-French war which began in 1337.[1] By early 1346, the war had brought mixed fortunes for the English. They had done better than most might have expected, but the record of success in battle was not startling. The initial years, 1337-9, had seen what amounted to little more than a phoney war. Diplomatic manoeuvring and a great deal of money had enabled Edward III and his advisers to build up a grand alliance against the French, an alliance in which the most important members were princes in the Low Countries and the emperor, Ludwig IV of Germany. The French, naturally, had countered this with similar activity, also acquiring support in the Low Countries, and, threateningly, Scotland. But it was one thing to create an alliance, and quite another to swing it into action. Edward's frustration during his long and expensive stay in the Low Countries cannot have been eased when in 1339 the two armies, the French and that of the English king and his allies,

---

[1] The fullest recent account of the war up to 1347 is by J. Sumption, *The Hundred Years War* (London, 1990). The most recent account of the Battle of Neville's Cross itself is in K. de Vries, *Infantry Warfare in the Early Fourteenth Century* (Woodbridge, 1996), pp. 176–87.

finally faced each other at Buironfosse. As so often happened, discretion had the better part of valour. Each army established a strong defensive position; neither was prepared to advance, and both withdrew from the battlefield at dusk. The next year, 1340, the English were more successful, with the naval victory at Sluys, but it was not followed up with any successful engagement on land. The siege of Tournai ended in disarray among the English allies, and once again the French avoided battle.

The next phase of the French war took place in Brittany. On 29 September 1343 the English defeated Charles of Blois, the French claimant to the duchy, at the Battle of Morlaix. The English under the Earl of Northampton took up a strong defensive position, protected by woods, and by trenches and pits dug by the troops. French cavalry troops failed to break through the English lines, and suffered grievous casualties. Northampton then withdrew: this was a minor and qualified victory, but it did demonstrate the effectiveness of English tactics. Historians have argued that war is about much more than battles, and they are quite right. The strategies of the Hundred Years War depended to a considerable extent on the destruction of enemy territory as a means of putting pressure on opponents, and in this regard, the English had certainly more than held their own in the initial phase of the French war. There was, however, little in what had happened between 1337 and 1345 to suggest the triumphs that were about to come.

A new phase of the war began in 1346, when the English invaded Normandy, sacked Caen, moved on up the Seine valley, and crossed the river near Paris. The French pursued them northwards; at Crécy on 26 August Edward III was victorious over Philip VI's army, and he was then free to move on to the siege of Calais. He had recruited a massive army, which would total some 30,000 in all, one of the largest armies ever assembled by a medieval English ruler.[2] The French needed assistance in the war, and naturally begged their Scottish allies for help. The opportunity presented to the Scots was a splendid one. The autumn was just the right time for a massive raid into England; the barns would still be full from the harvest, the beasts fat from the summer's grazing. The precedents for a Scottish invasion of England must have seemed encouraging. In Edward II's reign repeated raids had provided a steady source of income and plunder for the Scots. Resistance in 1319 from a motley army collected together by the Archbishop of York had culminated in Scottish victory at the Battle (or Chapter, as it was known) of Myton, near York. In 1322 Edward II's army was, if not defeated, at least thoroughly embarrassed by

[2]   A. Ayton, 'The English Army and the Normandy Campaign of 1346', in *England and Normandy in the Middle Ages*, ed. D. Bates and A. Curry (Woodbridge, 1994), pp. 266–7.

the Scots near Byland Abbey. When the Scots invaded in 1327, they were pursued in Weardale by a substantial English force, but the latter was unable to bring them to battle, and the campaign ended as a dismal, rain-soaked fiasco for the young Edward III. The omens in 1346 must have appeared very favourable to the ambitious David II. Above all, with Edward III and his chief nobles in France, there can have been no expectation of meeting any effective opposition.

The English were well aware of the possibility of trouble in the north in 1346. Orders went out at the start of the year for men to be recruited and arrayed to deal with a threatened Scottish invasion. On 8 March the Archbishop of York, the Bishop of Durham, Henry Percy, Ralph Neville and Thomas de Rokeby, sheriff of Yorkshire, were put in charge of the arrangements for defence. In the same month, Maurice de Berkeley was sent to York to discuss the safe custody of the northern marches with the local magnates.[3] Alan de Clavering went south to see the king on unspecified business concerning the north, and Thomas de Rokeby also went to see Edward about the custody of the northern March. Two clerks, Henry de Melbourne and William de Burton, went to London from the north between 19 August and 7 September, again about the affairs of the March. Espionage was as much a part of medieval as of modern warfare. Henry Percy was ordered by the king to send spies into Scotland, and William Snowe and a companion were sent from Ripon to try to discover what the Scots were doing.[4] The recruitment of troops did not go easily. There was difficulty in persuading the men of Nottinghamshire and Derbyshire to co-operate, and a commission was set up to deal with those who deserted, and those who refused to pay any contribution towards the costs of the men who were recruited.[5]

There were understandable hopes that the news of the English triumph at Crécy would persuade the Scots that they should agree to a truce. This may explain why the Scottish invasion seems to have taken the English by surprise when it began on 7 October. The Scots entered England in the west, rather than taking one of the more normal eastern routes. The Peel of Liddel was besieged and taken. Its keeper, Walter de Selby, was executed on David II's orders; to the Scots, he was a traitor, since earlier in his career, during Edward II's reign, he had sided with them. The citizens of Carlisle bought a truce from the Scots, buying peace for themselves and the western marches for three hundred marks. The Scots therefore marched

---

[3] *Rot. Scot.*, I, 668–71.

[4] London, Public Record Office, E 101/25/10 (Document i). Unfortunately these entries are undated, with the exception of Melbourne and Burton's mission. The instruction to Percy was issued on 22 August: *Rot. Scot.*, I, 674.

[5] Ibid., p. 673.

east to Hexham, where they spent three days doing much damage, and then moved on towards Durham, burning and pillaging in time-honoured fashion as they went. On 16 October they spent the night at the Prior of Durham's manor at Bearpark, from where plundering parties were sent out. According to the prior, they destroyed all the grain they found at Bearpark, killed or drove off all the animals, and cut down the trees in the park, doing over £100 worth of damage.[6]

In accordance with the plans made earlier in the year, responsibility for gathering forces to oppose the Scots was taken by the Archbishop of York, William Zouche; the Sheriff of Yorkshire, Thomas Rokeby, also had an important part to play. Ralph Neville, Henry Percy, Peter de Maulay and other northern nobles all assisted in the process. The initial muster was at Richmond; the army then marched to Barnard Castle, where it spent some time encamped at Eggleston Abbey just outside the town, causing considerable damage to the monks' property.[7] The decision was then taken to move on to Bishop Auckland in the hope of intercepting the Scots.

What kind of army was it that the English gathered together to oppose this invasion? Was it the case that success was achieved because of changes in methods of recruitment and organisation? This was a period of innovation and argument over the question of how armies should be recruited. In the early fourteenth century cavalry and infantry forces had been enlisted quite separately. Pay accounts show that they were organised in the field in totally different ways, with the cavalry serving in retinues of varying size and composition, and the infantry in standardised units of twenties and hundreds. One important change came in the 1330s, with the introduction of 'mounted archers', men who fought on foot, but rode to battle. Increasingly, in the early years of the Hundred Years War, these men were integrated into the cavalry retinues, so that great men provided not only knights and men-at-arms in their followings, but also archers. Contracts with commanders became more and more important; the Scottish expedition of 1337 provides the first example of an army wholly recruited by means of such contracts or indentures. Contract provided a secure financial basis for recruitment. However, there was still a concern to establish an effective system of military obligation, to ensure that men served when they were needed; the traditional feudal summons, by now wholly obsolete, had last been used in 1327. In 1346 Edward III tried to recruit men for the French campaign by means of a new scheme whereby landowners were obliged to provide troops according to the value of their estates. In the spring commissioners were appointed to recruit troops on this basis in the south of England for service in France. These measures

---

[6]   DCDCM, Reg ii, fol. 130v.
[7]   *CPR 1345–48*, p. 452.

were extremely unpopular, and had not Edward won the great victory at Crécy, it seems likely that he would have faced fierce opposition.[8]

For the Neville's Cross campaign, there was no attempt to innovate, and recruitment appears to have followed very orthodox lines. The obligation on men to serve in defence of the country in time of emergency was an ancient tradition. Where defence against invasion was concerned, there could be none of the possible constitutional objections that might be raised against service overseas. In March, the king had ordered proclamations to be made in Yorkshire, Durham and Northumberland, requiring all men between the ages of sixteen and sixty who were capable of bearing arms to be arrayed for the defence of the North. Those who were too sick or feeble were to provide substitutes. The order covered knights, other men-at-arms, lightly armed cavalry, known as hobelars, archers and others.[9] In practice, the recruitment of cavalry and infantry probably proceeded on rather different lines. Much of the cavalry was provided by the great lords. There can have been little difficulty in obtaining their co-operation. Unfortunately, there is little evidence from the Neville's Cross campaign to show how large the contingents provided by the magnates were, or even whether they were paid. Accounts from other campaigns help to show how many men they were capable of providing. In 1336 Ralph Neville called on the service of sixty-seven men-at-arms for the Scottish campaign of that year. In Flanders in the late 1330s his retinue consisted of one banneret, fourteen knights, and sixty-nine squires; he also had thirty mounted archers. Henry Scrope, in contrast, had no more than five squires with him. At the same period Henry Percy had a retinue of nineteen knights and eighty-seven men-at-arms serving in the north of England and Scotland. A bishop could collect together a very reasonable force: the Bishop of Carlisle provided four knights and fifty-two men-at-arms for eighteen days campaigning in Scotland in 1340.[10]

The system by which archers and other infantry troops were collected together by specially appointed arrayers had been developed in the thirteenth century. The question of the degree to which the local communities should support troops had long been a matter of argument, but there were conventions that a county should pay wages at least within

---

[8] M. R. Powicke, *Military Obligation in Medieval England* (Oxford, 1962), pp. 196–7.

[9] *Rot. Scot.*, I, 669.

[10] *The Wardrobe Book of William de Norwell 12 July 1338 to 27 May 1340*, ed. M. Lyon, B. Lyon, H. S. Lucas, J. de Sturler (Brussels, 1983), pp. 335, 342, 346, 354, and 362. Further, similar, figures are provided by A. Ayton, *Knights and Warhorses. Military Service and the English Aristocracy under Edward III* (Woodbridge, 1995), pp. 171–2.

its own boundaries, or until the troops mustered under the charge of a royal paymaster.[11] Thereafter the Crown would meet the costs of the campaign. Fortunately, for the Neville's Cross army there survives an account roll which provides much information about the troops involved. The account of John de Wodehouse shows how he spent the receipts from the north of two taxes, an income tax of a tenth paid by the clergy, and a fifteenth and tenth levied from the laity. It covers the period from 7 June 1345 to Michaelmas 1347. The total he had at his disposal came to £14,174 7s. 6¾d. Wodehouse's account covered much more than the Neville's Cross army. Large sums were due to John de Stirling, keeper of Berwick, who was owed £937 17s. for each quarter of the year; he was succeeded by Thomas de Musgrave who received 500 marks a quarter. John de Tiptoft was retained with a force of twenty men-at-arms and twenty archers for a year, and was paid almost £2,600. The defeat of the Scots at Neville's Cross was, in financial terms, a bargain in comparison. A contingent of sixty-four men-at-arms, of whom four were knights, came from Lancashire, with 640 mounted archers and 240 foot archers, and was paid just over £100 for the period from 13 October to 17 October; the men had already received wages for eight days service from their local communities. Some of them came well equipped and received a bonus of £20 in recognition. Fifteen men-at-arms with twenty-nine hobelars, or lightly armed cavalry, came with 3,020 archers from Yorkshire to the battle. Again, they received a week's wages from their localities, and were paid £207 4s. 8d. for 12 October to 16 October. It is curious that these men were not paid for the day of the battle itself. It is conceivable that they did not reach the battlefield in time, but perhaps more likely that they departed in too much haste to wait to be paid. Wodehouse himself had a small force of six men-at-arms and a dozen mounted archers, which he needed to keep guard over the money which he took from York to the battlefield in a cart hauled by five horses.[12]

These figures give some indication of how large the English forces at Neville's Cross army may have been. It would be reasonable to suppose that the magnates provided a total of at least a thousand men, and probably more, for the army. The *Anonimalle Chronicle* suggests that there were eight hundred men-at-arms present, and unlike most estimates given by chronicles, this seems very plausible. A newsletter written by a clerk, Thomas Samson, has a similar estimate of a thousand men-at-arms. The archers and common soldiers probably numbered some 5,000. A total of about 6,000 is much less than the figures given by contemporary authors: the writer of the *Anonimalle Chronicle* thought that the hobelars, archers and ordinary infantry totalled 10,000, while Samson considered that there were

[11] Powicke, *Military Obligation in Medieval England,* pp. 129, 137, 204, and 206.
[12] London, Public Record Office, E 101/25/10.

1,000 hobelars, 10,000 archers and 20,000 others.[13] Such figures, however, were commonly exaggerated.

An army of 6,000 may seem small, and so it was in comparison with the force of some 30,000 men that the king was able to deploy in the course of the campaign in France that saw the victory of Crécy and the siege of Calais. Such large armies were exceptional indeed. In Brittany in 1342 the English forces numbered some 1,900 men-at-arms, 1,890 mounted archers and 1,150 footsoldiers.[14] The Agincourt army probably numbered no more than about 8,000. In the conditions of the autumn of 1346 it simply would not have been possible or practicable to assemble a very large force to oppose the Scots.

What sort of tactics would the English use? It was in the earlier Scottish wars that the methods were developed which were to prove so successful in English hands in the Hundred Years War. The disastrous defeat of the English at Bannockburn in 1314 had shown how ineffective well-armed cavalry forces might be against well-positioned infantry, formed up in solid defensive formations known as schiltroms. The point was further emphasised at Boroughbridge in 1322, when the rebel Earl of Lancaster was defeated by royalist forces under Andrew Harclay which deliberately adopted Scottish tactics of fighting on foot. Harclay, veteran of border warfare, organised his men into schiltroms, though in fact these were scarcely needed in what amounted to little more than a skirmish in which Lancaster's men were prevented from crossing the Ouse. By 1327 the English were prepared to fight in a new style, with their men-at-arms dismounted. The young Edward III's first sight of troops drawn up for battle was on the campaign in Weardale that year; the boy king was led on his horse along the lines of dismounted knights, sergeants and squires. No doubt to his bitter disappointment, the Scots on that occasion were not prepared to move from their strong position on high ground. The English were not able to engage them, so the new tactics were not tested. Their effectiveness was soon proved beyond doubt in two battles in Scotland, at Dupplin Moor in 1332 and Halidon Hill, in the next year. English forces, formed up in a strong defensive position with ample support from archers, proved too much for the Scots. In France, the English lined up to fight in similar fashion on foot at Buironfosse in 1339, but, as on the Weardale campaign of 1327, no battle took place. There was a strong hint of how effective these tactics would be against the French at the Battle of Morlaix in 1342, but they were not proved in a major battle in the French war until 26 August 1346, when the Battle of Crécy was fought. English archers

---

[13] Documents b and d.

[14] M. C. Prestwich, *Armies and Warfare in the Middle Ages: The English Experience* (New Haven and London, 1996), p. 117; Ayton, *Knights and Warhorses*, p. 181.

shooting from defensive positions wrought havoc among their opponents. Initially it was Genoese crossbowmen who were driven off by the ferocious shooting of the English longbowmen; the latter then caused havoc among the French cavalry who followed in wave upon wave. In the hand-to-hand fighting which followed the English men-at-arms had a decisive advantage. The men who fought the Scots two months later certainly knew what had happened at Crécy in some detail, for John Neville, son of Ralph Neville, was present at both engagements. The expectation, therefore, would be that the English would draw up their troops in a strong defensive position, with archers on the flanks of the battalions of men-at-arms. The aim was to force an approaching enemy to fight on a relatively narrow front, so nullifying any advantage they might have in numerical terms.

Surprisingly, perhaps, the triumph at Neville's Cross was not very well served by contemporary writers. One of the problems with explaining medieval battles is that the sources are not, as a rule, very reliable. It would have been very hard for anyone to reconstruct the events of a battle accurately. Even commanders must often have had little idea of what was going on once an engagement had started; to build up a full picture would have necessitated interviewing participants on both sides in a way inconceivable for a medieval chronicler. Of course there were some battles described by participants, most notably Agincourt. Three major accounts of the English victory there were the work of eyewitnesses. This was exceptional. More common were newsletters sent back from campaign, and these rarely provided the sort of detail about battle tactics and fighting methods that historians would like to have. Accounts are frequently inconsistent and irreconcilable; military historians have had to resort to such questionable concepts as Colonel A. H. Burne's 'doctrine of military probability' to try to make sense of them.[15]

One answer to the problem of describing Neville's Cross was to be inventive. Jean le Bel, the Hainaulter who had described in vivid detail the 1327 Weardale campaign in which he took part, clearly felt that he understood English affairs sufficiently well that imagination could take the place of factual knowledge. According to him the queen went to Newcastle, where she was joined by the Archbishops of Canterbury and York, the Bishops of Lincoln and Durham, and a number of lay nobles. The English army numbered 1,200 horse, 5,000 archers (presumably mounted) and 8,000 infantry. The force was addressed by the queen, who then appointed commanders. She was taken into the castle at Newcastle. The battle then took place outside the walls: heroic and chivalric deeds took place, reminiscent of those of Roland and Oliver. The Earl of Buchan was killed,

---

[15] A. H. Burne, 'The Battle of Neville's Cross', *Durham University Journal*, new series 10 (1948–9), p. 105.

and the King of Scots captured by a valiant squire, John de Chappellein. So delighted was the queen by the victory that she kissed all her people, one after the other. The captor of the Scottish king initially did not give up David to the queen, but took him to his castle. John was then sent for by the king, who made him a knight and promised him £500 worth of land, and membership of the royal household, provided he handed over the Scottish ruler.[16] It all makes, as Jean le Bel intended, a splendid read: but it bears little relationship to the truth. Apart from anything else, the queen was in Ypres, in Flanders, when the battle took place outside Durham, not Newcastle. Regrettably, this account was used by Froissart as the basis for his account of the battle; a totally unreliable tradition was given unwarranted publicity.[17]

Other accounts are more plausible. It is possible to move behind the chronicle versions of events, for there are two surviving newsletters, one from Prior Fossor, who probably observed the battle from a safe distance, and one from Thomas Samson, clerk, canon of York and Beverley, who described the battle to his friends, probably within a week or so of the event. He may have been an eyewitness, but more probably relied on informants. The *Lanercost Chronicle* shared a common source, almost certainly another newsletter, with the *Anonimalle Chronicle*. Other chroniclers, such as Geoffrey le Baker, or the author of the *Meaux Chronicle*, were less inventive than le Bel and Froissart. A fifteenth-century Scottish chronicle, the *Scotichronicon*, may seem too late to be trustworthy, but contains some details which appear to be reliable. It is similar to the earlier work of Andrew Wyntoun, who wrote in the 1420s; both made use of a lost Latin chronicle probably written in the 1390s. The various accounts contradict each other too often to make a completely convincing reconstruction of the battle possible.[18]

Even the site of the battle presents problems. Its location was made known in advance by St Cuthbert in a convenient vision;[19] but the saint has not been so obliging to later historians. In his letter, Prior Fossor described the Scots drawn up in battle formation on the moor of Bearpark, next to the park itself. He also described the battle as taking place between Durham City and Findon Hill. The *Anonimalle Chronicle* described the Scots moving out from Bearpark, with both armies then assembling at Neville's Cross. The *Meaux Chronicle* places the battle on the moor between Durham

[16] *Jean le Bel*, II, 127–31.
[17] Remarkably, de Vries, *Infantry Warfare*, p. 181, gives some credence to Froissart's account of Queen Philippa's involvement in the battle.
[18] Documents a–h.
[19] *Chronica monasterii de Melsa a fundatione usque ad annum 1396*, ed. E. A. Bond (RS 43; 3 vols., London, 1866–8), III, 62 (Document e).

and Bearpark, with each army occupying strong positions on high ground, set a quarter of a mile apart. The *Scotichronicon* has the English army drawn up close to Neville's Cross: one of the difficulties facing the armies was the hedges and ditches crossing the site. Both armies are likely to have taken up strong defensive positions, but where precisely on the undulating high ground has to remain uncertain. As Colonel A.H. Burne observed, 'there is of course ample evidence that the battle took place on the ridge to the west of the city. But almost any point on this ridge from near Bearpark to the cross ridge just south of Neville's Cross could be reconciled with the statements of the chroniclers.' He also noted that it was curious that there was no mention made of the ridge itself, or of the Browney valley. This did not deter him. Armed with the doctrine of inherent military probability, he provided a map showing the disposition of the troops on both sides. The English, he was clear, were drawn up three hundred yards in front of the Cross, with the Browney valley to their left.[20] Such certainty is unwise; inherent military probability is a dangerous weapon, for war is full of improbabilities. All one can safely do is identify the general area in which the battle took place, lying to the north or north-west of Neville's Cross, and note that commanders might show a preference for a site defended on either side by natural features. In this case, the steep fall down to the Browney valley on the west, and to Flass Vale on the east, surely helped to define the best place for establishing a defensive line.

The events that preceded the battle, and its timing, also present problems. The Scots were at Bearpark on 16 October, and spent the night before the battle there. According to the *Lanercost Chronicle*, at dawn on the day of the battle William Douglas left the Scottish camp at Bearpark to ravage the countryside. At Merrington he and his foragers were shocked to encounter, looming up through dense fog, a substantial English army. Many Scots were killed in a swift engagement, but Douglas escaped. He returned to the camp and roused King David who must have been startled to learn that the English had been able to recruit an effective army. The Scots army duly assembled for battle. The account in the *Scotichronicon* is similar. On the morning of 17 October Douglas on his raiding party encountered English forces at Ferryhill, withdrew, but lost many of his men at Sunderland Bridge. It appears that the English army spent the night of 16 October in the bishop's park at Auckland. It was initially hoped to fight at Kirk Merrington, but then the force moved on to Sunderland Bridge, and then to the site of the battle. Prior Fossor has it that the troops faced each other on Bearpark Moor from Terce (about 8.30 a.m.) until Nones, when the fighting proper began. The related *Lanercost* and *Anonimalle Chronicles* also start the battle at Terce. Times, of course, were imprecise in this

---

[20]   Burne, 'The Battle of Neville's Cross', pp. 103 and 105.

period, changing with shifts in sunrise and sunset.[21] One theory resolves these problems of timing by placing the engagement with Douglas's force on 16 October, so enabling the battle proper to start early in the morning on the following day.[22] This runs in the face of the bulk of the evidence, and leaves the question of where the English spent the night of 16 October unanswered.

It makes more sense to place all the events on a single day. It was certainly not unknown for an army to start its march before daybreak; Edward I's army in 1298 began its march to the battlefield of Falkirk before dawn broke. There would have been sufficient time for a swift mounted march from Auckland at or before dawn, an early morning engagement near Sunderland Bridge, and a move on to Neville's Cross. Samson in his letter has the duration of the battle as from Nones to Vespers, that is, about 1.30 or 2.00 p.m until about 4.30 or 5.00 p.m. This would have put an immense physical strain on the troops, and the stamina of the men who achieved so much in a day must have been remarkable. This, however, is the scenario which fits the sources best.

The organisation of the two armies is relatively clear. Both were formed up in three 'battles'. This was normal practice. Samson gives some detail. Percy, Neville, Maulay, Scrope, Musgrave, with the Sheriff of Northumberland and Andrew FitzRalph were the bannerets in charge of the first. The second was led by the archbishop, the Earl of Angus, Lord Deyncourt, Roger la Zouche and Ralph Hastings, along with the Provost of Beverley. The third battle, the rearguard, was under Mowbray, Leyburn, and the Sheriff of Yorkshire. The *Anonimalle* chronicler gives as much detail, but predictably his account differs in some specifics. Samson's second 'battle' is his third; the Earl of Angus features in his list of the first 'battle'. The archers receive little mention, for all that they were undoubtedly far more numerous than the men-at-arms. The Meaux chronicler, however, places them on the flanks, which is surely correct.

There is relatively little detail provided about the actual fighting. The *Meaux Chronicle* has a story which rings true, of an initial attack on the Scottish position by a group of English archers. Geoffrey le Baker explained that the English archery was less effective than usual, though the *Scotichronicon* noted that Sir John Graham, earl of Menteith, failed to persuade any of the Scots cavalry to join him in an attempt to break up the lines of English archers. Fear of the effects of English arrows must have been potent. However, the Scots in tight infantry formation — the famous schiltroms — with their helmets and shields carefully positioned, were

---

[21] Times in the medieval period are discussed by M. D. Knowles, *The Monastic Order in England 943–1216* (Cambridge, 1941), pp. 448–53 and 714–15.

[22] W. Brown, 'Neville's Cross', *Ushaw Magazine* 1 (1891), pp. 220–2.

probably not so vulnerable to the longbow as were Scottish or French cavalry. After the initial manoeuvring, the two armies engaged, on foot, in hand-to-hand combat. The English were forced back at least once. Once, if not twice or even three times, the exhausted troops on both sides laid down their weapons. A half-time break may be usual in football matches, but was an unusual feature of a medieval battle. At least two whirlwind attacks by the English took place. The *mêlée* was clearly hard-fought on all sides. When at last it seemed to them that the battle was lost, Patrick, earl of Dunbar, and the Steward, who were in charge of the Scottish rearguard, took to flight. The effect of this on the morale of the Scots still fighting must have been devastating. The *mêlée* soon turned to a rout. It would surely have been at this stage that the English would have called up their horses. The Scots were driven from the battlefield, northwards towards Sacriston during the fading light of evening.

In the closing stages of the battle King David of Scotland was captured. He was wounded by two arrows, and was taken by John de Coupland, a Northumberland man. In the struggle, Coupland lost two teeth to a blow from the king's gauntleted fist, or so the *Scotichronicon* has it. There is no suggestion here that the king was fleeing: he was cornered between some ditches. Geoffrey le Baker has the king captured in a heroic last stand on the field of battle. The *Meaux Chronicle's* account is that he was in flight; that may tally with that least reliable but most picturesque of sources, local tradition. It is said that King David was caught by Coupland who saw his reflection as he hid under a bridge, probably that at Aldingrange. It is possible that the king was trying to escape on the flank of the fighting, along the Browney valley, but there can be no proof. Documentary sources support the chronicle accounts, and show that the king was indeed wounded by archery in the course of the battle. Those wounds did not prove too serious, but it was necessary to send for two barber surgeons from York, William de Bolton and Hugh de Kilnyngton, to come to Bamburgh to extract an arrow from the unfortunate Scottish king. According to Froissart, David still had a fragment of an arrowhead in his head in 1365, which gave him severe headaches when the moon was new.[23]

* * * * *

News of the victory spread rapidly. The government in London issued letters on 20 October, announcing the triumph and giving what was considered to be due credit to God for ensuring that right and justice had

---

[23] *CPR 1345–48*, pp. 225–6 and 552; *CCR 1346–49*, pp. 306, 477, and 547 (E 101/25/10); *Scotichronicon by Walter Bower in Latin and English*, ed. D. R. Watt *et al.* (Aberdeen and Edinburgh, 1987–), VII, 464.

triumphed. The undoubted euphoria did not blind the authorities to the deficiences of the recruitment process; on 4 November Henry Percy, Ralph Neville, Thomas de Rokeby and others were commissioned to find out who had failed to do their public duty. There was then much business to be done to get the Scottish prisoners brought to London; then the business of arranging ransoms could begin in earnest.[24]

This was not a battle won by any single masterly stroke of generalship. It certainly does not appear that any one bold tactical move was important in achieving victory; no doubt the use of the tactics tried and tested at Crécy was important, but the indications are that it was above all hard hand-to-hand fighting that won the battle. In France the importance of the archers was very clear, but the accounts do not suggest that their role was as decisive at Neville's Cross. One interpretation has it that they 'proved very capable in narrowing the charge of the Scottish force', but there is no evidence for this.[25] The character of the ground alone surely prevented the Scots from making flanking attacks, or from advancing on a very broad front. The victory was achieved, not so much by archery, as by the hard work of fighting hand-to-hand in a fierce *mêlée*. This was an exceptionally hard- fought engagement, which richly deserved what almost amounts to poetry used by the author of the *Lanercost Chronicle*. No translation can do this justice, with its alliteration and rhyme;

> tubis clangentibus, scutis concurrentibus, sagittis volantibus, hastis perforantibus, percussis proclamantibus, et turmis ululantibus, armis penetratis, capitibus conquassatis, pluribus, proh dolor! in campo prostratis.[26]

The battle was as much a triumph for the ordinary soldiers who took part, as for the Archbishop of York and the nobles. Grants made after the battle show that in some cases it was men of no great rank who took notable Scots prisoner. The greatest triumph, of course, was that of the northern squire John de Coupland, who took David II himself captive.[27]

A final question concerns the role of the Durham monks during the battle. According to Knighton, a late and not very reliable source, the monks took to the top of the cathedral tower (which did not stand as high as it does today), and filled the air with bells ringing, singing, shouting and weeping as they saw the Scots flee.[28] The more romantic tale is that St

---

[24] *Rot. Scot.*, I, 675 and 677–81.

[25] de Vries, *Infantry Warfare*, p. 187.

[26] *Lanercost*, p. 351.

[27] *CCR 1346–49*, pp. 305–6 and 547. For a list of those taken, see *Rot. Scot.*, I, 678. See below, pp. 36–48.

[28] *Chronicon Henrici Knighton, vel Cnitthon, monachi Leycestrensis*, ed. J. R. Lumby (RS 92; 2 vols., London, 1889–95), II, 42–3.

Cuthbert instructed, by means of a vision, the Prior of Durham to take the cloth which the saint had used to cover the chalice when he said Mass, to put it on the point of a spear, and to go to the site of the battle until it ended. The prior and his monks duly set out, and took up station on the Maiden's Bower, a prehistoric barrow which lies down in Flass Vale, well below the ridge on which the battle was fought. Many Scots ran by them, but they were protected by God, St Cuthbert, and the relic with them, so no violence was done to them. This comes not from a contemporary source, but from unattributed local tradition. Colonel Burne, here clearly relying on a doctrine of military improbability, used this evidence to suggest that the monks on the Maiden's Bower were behind the Scottish lines. He also suggested that this group were signalling to their colleagues on the cathedral tower to indicate how the battle was going. It may be that the prior and his monks were as foolish as this story suggests, but the lines of sight do not fit the topography, and the tale does not ring true.[29]

The theory that decisive battles have determined the course of history is no longer popular, but the importance of Neville's Cross cannot be denied. It is perhaps unlikely that defeat for the English would have resulted in David extending his kingdom as far as the Humber, as one account reported his ambition. Yet defeat would have been a major blow to Edward III and his ambitions in France. His reign would have taken a very different, and surely far less successful course. 1347 would have been a year of political crisis, and would not have witnessed the triumph of the capture of Calais. Relations between England and Scotland would have been very different; Edward III's attentions would have been focused upon the Scottish, rather than the French, war, and it is likely that success for the Scots at Neville's Cross would have resulted in many more years of bitter Anglo-Scottish conflict.[30]

---

[29] Surtees, I, lii; Burne, 'Battle of Neville's Cross', pp. 104–6.

[30] I am extremely grateful to Mrs E. Offler and Mr A. Piper for allowing me to see the notes for a lecture that the late Professor H. S. Offler gave on the narrative sources for the battle. I also owe a debt of gratitude to Professor Clifford J. Rogers, both for his helpful comments and for sight of an article he has written on Neville's Cross.

Disaster at Neville's Cross: The Scottish Point of View

ALEXANDER GRANT

In his *Orygynale Cronykil of Scotland*, which was finally completed in about 1420, Prior Andrew Wyntoun of Lochleven reflected sadly on David II's decision to invade England in October 1346.

> Quhy couth he nocht haif bene in pess,
> And reullit his land in richtiusnes,
> And haldin him self out of dangere?
> Quha standis weile, he suld nocht steire.[1]

In other words, things that are going well should not be disturbed. Wyntoun answered his question by explaining that the Scots were far too confident that the good fortune they had enjoyed over the past five or so years would continue – but forgot that Fortune's wheel always turns. That is, of course, post-battle hindsight. Yet, as we shall see, by 1346, after fifty years of bitter conflict, the Scots did seem at last to have won their long war with England, and to have maintained their independence successfully. So Wyntoun's question is certainly valid: in 1346, what need was there for the Scottish invasion?

To answer, the 1346 situation must be put into the context of half a century of Anglo-Scottish hostility.[2] This had originated in the Scottish

---

[1] *The Original Chronicle of Andrew of Wyntoun*, ed. F. J. Amours (Scottish Text Society; 6 vols., 1903–14), VI, 170; translation as Document h, below. There, Wyntoun's spelling and some of his words have been modernised; but the passages quoted in my text have been left essentially as printed by Amours, except that I have rendered 'þ', 'ß' and 'ȝ' as 'th', 'ss' and 'y' respectively. Specific page-references are not given for quotations from any of the passages from chronicles, etc., printed in the Appendix.

[2] For brief general accounts of the Anglo-Scottish warfare, see M. Lynch, *Scotland: A New History* (2nd edn, London, 1992); A. Grant, *Independence and Nationhood: Scotland, 1306–1469* (London, 1984), chs. 1–2; and R. Nicholson, *Scotland: The Later Middle Ages* (Edinburgh, 1974), chs. 2–6. Detailed accounts of the earlier stages are given in G. W. S. Barrow, *Robert Bruce and the Community of the Realm of Scotland* (3rd edn, Edinburgh, 1988); and R. Nicholson, *Edward III and the Scots* (Oxford, 1965) (though that only goes to 1335). See also J. Campbell, 'England, Scotland and the Hundred Years War', in *Europe in the Late Middle Ages*, ed. J. R. Hale *et al.* (London, 1965), pp. 184–216.

succession crisis that followed the death of Alexander III in 1286. The royal family's direct line finally came to an end in 1290, by which time its two leading cadets, John Balliol of Galloway and Robert Bruce of Annandale, were bitterly disputing the succession. To prevent the incipient civil war, Edward I of England was asked to adjudicate between them. He found, correctly, for John Balliol – but he made the Scots recognise himself as overlord of Scotland. In 1295, however, his demands for Scottish military service against France were refused, and instead the Scots allied with the French. That led to war between Scotland and England in 1296. Edward defeated the Scots, removed King John from the throne, and imposed direct rule from Westminster. But in 1297 widespread rebellion took place, under, most famously, William Wallace and Andrew Murray; this brought six more years of war on behalf of the exiled John Balliol, until in 1304 most Scots finally submitted to Edward. In 1306, however, there was a new rebellion. This time the Scots were led by Robert Bruce, grandson of the claimant of 1290; he had himself made king, as Robert I. But in his *coup d'état*, Bruce had killed John Comyn, head of Scotland's most powerful family and John Balliol's main supporter. The Balliol/Comyn faction therefore became Robert's implacable foes, and the threatened Bruce–Balliol civil war finally broke out – conjointly with Bruce's war against the English. Naturally the Balliol/Comyn faction sided with the English, and, to begin with, Bruce's forces were routed. But after Edward I's death in 1307, English pressure slackened, and Robert was able to deal with his Scottish opponents. By 1309 he had defeated them in the North, and by late 1314, following his victory over Edward II at Bannockburn, he had gained full control of his kingdom (except for Berwick, then Scotland's leading town, which held out until 1318). But Edward II would not recognise Robert as king, nor agree to Scottish independence – so the war dragged on. The Scots took it to the English by invading Ireland and repeatedly raiding northern England. It was not, however, until after Edward II's deposition in 1327 that Robert, with a particularly spectacular set of attacks, managed to force a peace settlement from the English government of Isabella and Mortimer. Scotland's independence and Robert I's kingship were at last recognised formally, by the Treaty of Edinburgh of 1328.

Unfortunately, Robert I died a year later, in 1329. His son and successor, David II, was only five years old. Three years later, in 1332, the war started up again, with an attack by the exiled heirs of the Balliol/Comyn faction – egged on by Edward III, who had never accepted 'the shameful peace' of 1328. Not only Robert I but also his two great lieutenants, Thomas Randolph and James Douglas, had died; without them, the Scottish leadership proved incompetent. The invaders won a crushing victory at Dupplin (near Perth), and crowned Edward Balliol, the son of King John. Although they were subsequently driven out, they returned in force in 1333 – along with Edward III and a huge English host. Edward besieged Berwick – and the Scottish army which tried to relieve it was destroyed at Halidon Hill by his archers and men-at-arms. Many surviving Scots submitted; the young David II was sent for safety to France; Scotland seemed conquered again. Significantly, unlike his grandfather, Edward III did not try to take over the entire country; instead, he partitioned it. Edward Balliol was allowed to rule the North, under only nominal overlordship; while Edward III annexed most of the region south of the Forth. But this new policy was no more successful; again there was sporadic Scottish resistance, which gradually gained support. Edward III's grip on Scotland was no tighter than Edward I's – and in 1337 he turned his main attention away, to war against France. That war broke out largely because, under the terms of the Franco-Scottish alliance (confirmed by Robert I in 1326), the French had been giving vital support to David II's cause, even threatening to invade southern England: the Hundred Years War was essentially sparked off by the Franco-Scottish alliance.[3] But once Edward III's attention focused on France, the pressure on Scotland relaxed. David II's supporters steadily regained control over the kingdom; David came back from France in 1341, and by late 1342 almost all of Scotland was back under the Bruce regime's control. Once more, the war with England had been won. So – as Wyntoun asked – why did the Scots have to reopen it by attacking England in 1346?

This would, in fact, have made sense at the time, for various reasons. The first is that the whole of Scotland had not been liberated. Three major strongholds were still in English hands: Lochmaben Castle, in the south-west; Jedburgh Castle, in the central Borders; and the town of Berwick, with its castle, on the east coast. Moreover, despite the success of David II's supporters, Edward III refused to conclude a peace; instead, he still regarded Edward Balliol as King of Scots. Thus in 1342 the situation was the same as after Bannockburn, and so was the problem facing David II: how could he force the King of England to recognise Scotland's independence and the Bruce kingship? The basic point had been made in 1325, in a poem written by Robert I's chancellor, Abbot Bernard of Arbroath, to celebrate the birth of the future David II:

> He [David] will play at combat in the gardens of the English;
> Or else, may God make a lasting peace between the kingdoms.[4]

---

3 Cf. *ibid.*, pp. 189–91; and A. Curry, *The Hundred Years War* (Basingstoke, 1993), pp. 142–4.

4 *Scotichronicon by Walter Bower, in Latin and English*, ed. D. E. R. Watt *et al.*

In other words, lasting peace could only be achieved through Scottish military action in England: that was the situation in the 1320s, and now again in the 1340s.

A second reason is that – as the poem implies – his Scottish contemporaries would surely have expected David, as his father's son, to attack England. David, who was seventeen years old when he returned to Scotland in 1341, and only twenty-two at the time of Neville's Cross, had grown up in a militaristic atmosphere at Château Gaillard in Normandy, and throughout his life was just as keen on chivalry and chivalrous exploits as Edward III. But during his absence in France, Scotland had been liberated by various warlords who had fought without royal supervision, and, through their military successes, had become extremely powerful. After 1341, David had to deal with several magnates who seem distinctly over-mighty, and almost contemptuous towards crown authority.[5] The best way for David to assert that authority was to prove himself to be the mightiest Scottish warlord, like his father. And that required him to wage triumphant war in England, by leading powerful raids – as he duly did in 1342 and 1345. But a considerable task still lay before him in 1346, as is illustrated by the fact that at the September muster at Perth, William, earl of Ross, encountered his West-Highland rival Ranald MacRuari of Garmoran, promptly killed him, and then took his men home to Ross. Such outrageous behaviour would have been unthinkable under Robert I.

The third reason is that (as pointed out in the previous chapter) the fatal invasion was in response to appeals for help from Philip VI of France in June and July 1346,[6] when Edward III invaded Normandy. The Franco-Scottish Treaty had obliged the Scots to attack England in the event of Anglo-French war, in return for the promise of French aid during Anglo-Scottish war. The French king had kept his side of the bargain in the 1330s; now it was the turn of the King of Scots. It is inconceivable that David would have refused to honour the Scottish obligation. That was, indeed, as much in Scotland's interests as France's – increasingly so, as 1346 wore on. In August, Edward III defeated the French at Crécy, and proceeded to besiege Calais. Crécy raised the nightmare prospect for the Scots that the French would have to make peace with Edward III – and

---

5   (Aberdeen and Edinburgh, 1987–), VII, 14–15.

The significance of the local warlords, especially William Douglas of Liddesdale, is highlighted by M. H. Brown, 'The Development of Scottish Border Lordship, 1332–1358', *Historical Research* 70 (1997), pp. 1–22. There are obvious parallels with Edward III and Henry V, who both tackled English domestic political problems by campaigning in France – except that they were triumphantly successful.

6   Campbell, 'England, Scotland and the Hundred Years War', p. 195.

break the Franco-Scottish alliance. That would have let Edward III focus his whole attention on Scotland again, as in the mid-1330s. Obviously, therefore, the Scots had to do what they could to maintain their vital alliance with France. Thus in July 1346 a raid was launched across the western Border[7] – in instant response to the first French request. But as the year went on, it must have become clear not only that the crisis in France was getting much worse, but also that the siege of Calais required a very large English army – at over 30,000 men, the largest English army ever to campaign abroad during the middle ages. The Scots knew about that – and drew the wrong conclusion. Almost every source for Neville's Cross, whether Scottish or English, emphasises how the Scots believed that the whole of England had been stripped of fighting men, and that therefore they could invade northern England with impunity. In October 1346, David II and his commanders did not expect to meet any serious English opposition at all.

So – a fourth reason – the opportunity was simply too good to miss. It must be stressed again that, despite the wisdom of hindsight, the Neville's Cross invasion did make sense in terms of the Anglo-Scottish war, Scottish domestic politics, and the Franco-Scottish treaty. But it also made sense in cruder terms, those of cross-Border raiding. There is a long history, and a deep-rooted mythology, of Scottish raids into England, from Roman times to those of the Jacobites. And although, nowadays, people generally omit the third verse of the National Anthem, asking God to save the Queen from marauding Scots (it was written soon after 1745), the build-up to the 1996 England–Scotland football international at Wembley shows that the concept of the invading Scot devastating England is still very much alive, at least in the media. There were fears of Scottish hooligans terrorising London, and vivid recollections of the occasion in 1977 when the Wembley goalposts were burned and the pitch dug up. The fear of Scottish raids has sunk deeply into the English national psyche. This can easily be traced back to the middle ages – and, in particular, to the twelfth century. It was then, as John Gillingham has demonstrated, that a strong sense of Englishness developed, characterised in terms of English civilisation opposed to the barbarity of the other races of the British Isles.[8] That is because the practice of slave-raiding, which had previously been the normal method of waging war, had ceased in England but continued elsewhere – so that in the eleventh and twelfth centuries a civilised and superior England seemed to

---

[7] *Lanercost*, p. 341.

[8] J. Gillingham, 'Foundations of a Disunited Kingdom', in *Uniting the Kingdom? The Making of British History,* ed. A. Grant and K. J. Stringer (London, 1995), pp. 56–64; J. Gillingham, 'The Beginnings of English Imperialism', *Journal of Historical Sociology* 5 (1992), pp. 392–409.

have been under attack by uncivilised, slave-raiding, barbarians – especially Scots. And although Scotland's society and *mores* subsequently developed like England's, the English experience of Robert I's attacks in the years after Bannockburn naturally confirmed the idea of the 'barbarian' threat from north of the Border. The concept of Scottish 'barbarian' raids was, indeed, a major formative element in that powerful politico-historical force, the sense of English superiority which (the non-English would say) has so affected British, European and World history.

Yet – to return briefly to football – the supporters who are notorious for hooliganism are not the Scots but the English, and English complaints about Scottish football supporters are distinctly hypocritical. And the same applies to the medieval cross-Border raiding. No matter how much the north of England suffered at Scottish hands,[9] Scotland surely suffered much more from the English, especially during the Wars of Independence. These began, after all, with a very limited Scottish raid on the villages around Carlisle – to which Edward I retaliated by capturing Scotland's most important town, Berwick, and massacring its inhabitants.[10] There is no comparable atrocity in the history of the British Isles until Oliver Cromwell destroyed Drogheda. And no English town has ever suffered such a massacre. Consider, too, all the major English invasions of Scotland: under Edward I, in 1296, 1298, 1300, 1301, 1303–4 and 1307; under Edward II, in 1310–11, 1314 and 1322; and under Edward III (before Neville's Cross), in 1333, 1334, 1335, 1336, 1338 and 1341. Also, before 1346, there had already been four shattering Scottish defeats with terrible Scottish casualties: at Dunbar in 1296, Falkirk in 1298, Dupplin in 1332 and Halidon in 1333. The death-toll of Scottish magnates at English hands, in battle or on the scaffold, is horrendous: it includes, for instance, all Robert I's brothers, Edward, Thomas, Alexander and Nigel Bruce, plus his bastard son Robert; while the top layer of Scottish society also lost an Earl of Angus, two Earls of Atholl, two Earls of Carrick, an Earl of Lennox, an Earl of Mar, an Earl of Menteith, an Earl of Moray, an Earl of Ross, and an Earl of Sutherland.[11] The ranks of the Scottish baronage were similarly decimated. Finally, consider the material damage done throughout Scotland by the English invasions and countless lesser raids. The *Lanercost Chronicle*

---

[9]   R. Lomas, 'The Impact of Border Warfare: The Scots and South Tweedside, *c.*1290–*c.*1520', *Scottish Historical Review* 75 (1996), pp. 143–67, concludes that 'in the long run the frequency and scale of [the Scottish raids] were too limited to have had more than a marginal effect' on the economy of the Border area.

[10]   M. Prestwich, *Edward I* (London, 1988), pp. 470–1.

[11]   Details can be found in *The Scots Peerage*, ed. J. Balfour Paul (Edinburgh, 1904–14).

records, for example, that in August 1336 an English force 'marched ... into Carrick and the western parts of Scotland ... laying them waste as much as it could, burning and carrying away splendid spoil'.[12] That is one of nine virtually identical passages in the *Lanercost Chronicle* describing English devastation of substantial parts of Scotland between 1333 and 1337. And there had been much more of it earlier on. In view of all the sufferings that the Scots and Scotland had experienced at English hands during the previous fifty years, it can surely be suggested that the main, and most understandable, motivation for the Scottish invasion of 1346 would have been, quite simply, revenge.

Let us turn now to the actual campaign. Because Scottish armies were unpaid, there is not the kind of data that has allowed English historians to analyse the English war machine so brilliantly. So far as David's army is concerned, the English government believed that he was recruiting as many men as possible, 'from the Isles as well as from other parts of Scotland',[13] and there can be no doubt that forces from the whole country were summoned to the muster, which was probably held north of the Forth, at Perth, some time in September.[14] But (as already seen) two Highland magnates who attended, the Earl of Ross and Ranald MacRuari, did not go on the campaign; and there is no evidence that the greatest Highlander of all, John MacDonald, lord of the Isles, took part.[15] On the other hand, the

---

[12] *Lanercost*, p. 287.

[13] *Rot. Scot.*, I, 672; the reference to recruitment from the Isles is perhaps an example of the barbarian motif.

[14] *Lanercost*, ed. Stevenson, p. 344, states that the Scots assembled on 6 October; but it is the date at which they assembled on and crossed the Border that is meant, not the muster at Perth recorded by Wyntoun. That muster could not have been on 6 October (as in Nicholson, *Later Middle Ages*, p. 146, and *Scotichronicon*, ed. Watt, VII, 253 and 459). The English government knew David was recruiting on 20 August: *Rot. Scot.*, I, 672. The last document issued by David II before the battle was dated at Stirling on 8 September; it gave Patrick Fleming the hereditary right to lead all the men of Tweeddale, and so was probably connected with the muster: *Regesta Regum Scottorum*, vol. VI: *The Acts of David II, King of Scots, 1329–1371*, ed. B. Webster (Edinburgh, 1982), no. 108. It seems unlikely, however, that the manpower of Lothian, Clydesdale and the Borders was ordered to go all the way north to Perth and then return south for the actual invasion; more probably there were separate musters for the regions south of the Forth, and the whole army may not have come together until it reached the Border. That is actually what Wyntoun tells us ('Quhare at the peill of Liddalisdaill / His oste till him assemblit haill'), and it is probably what the *Lanercost Chronicle's* statement means.

[15] The *Anonimalle Chronicle* (Document d) includes 'Ranald the Small, leader of the people of the Outer Isles' in its list of the invasion's leaders, but this is probably Ranald MacRuari; the Earl of Ross is also named in the list, so

Earls of Sutherland and Moray, and Robert Stewart, David's nephew and heir-apparent, who held the northern earldom of Atholl, certainly were present at Neville's Cross, presumably with men from those three Highland earldoms. That said, the lists of Scots who were killed or captured consist predominantly of men from the Borders, the South-West, Lothian, Fife and Central Scotland: there are very few from the northern half of the country (apart from the earls of Moray and Sutherland themselves).[16] So perhaps it actually was a mainly southern army. Alternatively, perhaps the northerners do not figure among the casualties because they were in the division commanded by Robert Stewart, which fled from the field.

How big was the Scottish army? There is only one usable indication. According to Wyntoun, when the Scots were at Hexham, the army was arrayed, 'And in till all thar ost thai fand / Off armyt men bot twa thowsande'. That does not mean, however, that there were only 2,000 in the army, as has sometimes been said. In one of the other main Scottish chronicles, the *Scotichronicon* of Walter Bower, abbot of Inchcolm (written in the 1440s), which at this point was independently using the same source as Wyntoun, the equivalent passage reads: 'and the total came to only about two thousand well-armed men, although the count included a great army of those that were lightly armed'. This surely records an actual count, and can probably be taken seriously. What it indicates is that David's army had a core of some 2,000 well-armed troops, and in addition a much larger number (many, perhaps, Highlanders) who were not well armed – who were along for the raid, so to speak. This division between a smallish effective core and a large ineffective fringe tallies well with A. A. M. Duncan's recent discussion of the make-up of the armies led by Robert I within Scotland.[17]

It may, however, be doubted that the 1346 army was like the forces that Robert I, James Douglas, and Thomas Randolph led in their raids on England. They commanded tightly controlled, fast-moving, efficient raiding parties, as Jean le Bel's eye-witness account of the Scottish attack on Weardale in 1327 demonstrates.[18] One of le Bel's most famous images is

---

presumably it derived from English intelligence about the original muster. John MacDonald did have a son called Ranald, but he was probably too young to have taken part in the campaign.

[16] That is the impression I have gained from the casualty lists given in the various accounts of the battle.

[17] A. A. M. Duncan, 'The War of the Scots, 1306–23', *Transactions of the Royal Historical Society*, 6th series, 2 (1992), pp. 144–6.

[18] *Jean le Bel*, I, 50–2. This part of Le Bel's chronicle can also be found incorporated into Froissart's *Chroniques*; see for example *Froissart, Chronicles*, trans. and ed. G. Brereton (Harmondsworth, 1968), pp. 46–54.

how the Scottish raiders, once they could no longer stomach half-cooked meat, lived off oatmeal flour which they carried with them and made into cakes on a stone griddle. The 1346 invasion was a very different affair. The *Lanercost Chronicle* states that David II 'strictly ordered that four northern towns should not be burnt, to wit, Hexham, Corbridge, Darlington and Durham, because he intended to obtain his victual from them'.[19] David was not going to eat half-cooked meat and oatcakes; he intended to live properly off the provisions that were to be found in northern England. That would have been much more palatable – but would have limited his army's mobility (as would the Scottish baggage, including what Thomas Sampson called 'tents and pavilions of the richest and noblest sort, the likes of which had not been seen in these parts for a long time').

The *Lanercost Chronicle's* statement that David forbade the burning of those four towns implies, moreover, that the Scots were not simply mounting a mindless plundering raid. This is corroborated by other English chronicles. One recorded that the Carlisle region bought off a Scottish attack by paying 300 marks (£200), while another said that before the battle Durham was negotiating to do likewise, for the sum of £1,000.[20] Those are the kind of amounts that Robert I was extorting in 'protection money' from northern English communities in the years after Bannockburn. The standard study of Robert's raiding, indeed, concludes that he was more interested in getting cash than 'inanimate booty', though he also took much cattle. And Duncan argues that levying cash was actually the main aim of the Scottish raids, especially before 1318, because Robert needed it to pay the costs of his campaigns.[21] Something similar could have been in David II's mind when he crossed the Border on 7 October 1346. Be that as it may, it must be reiterated that the Scots did not expect to meet any serious opposition – which probably explains why the October invasion seems fairly leisurely, and the army distinctly flabby.

That brings us to the battle itself. In the previous chapter Michael Prestwich has rightly pointed out that 'the various accounts contradict each other too often to make a completely convincing reconstruction of the battle possible'. The contemporary English letters and chronicles are impressionistic, giving relatively little detail about what was obviously a complex sequence of engagements; and it is particularly unfortunate that the account of these years written by Sir Thomas Grey of Heton, a

---

[19] *Lanercost*, p. 346.
[20] *The Anonimalle Chronicle*, ed. V. H. Galbraith (Manchester, 1927), p. 24; *Chronicon Henrici Knighton, vel Cnitthon, monachi Leycestrensis*, ed. J. R. Lumby (RS 92; 2 vols., London, 1889–95), II, 41.
[21] J. Scammell, 'Robert I and the North of England', *English Historical Review* 73 (1958), pp. 385-403; Duncan, 'War of the Scots', pp. 147–8.

Northumbrian who may have fought there himself and knew many who certainly did, has been lost from his *Scalacronica*. On the other hand, the Scottish chronicles by Prior Wyntoun and Abbot Bower do provide more of a narrative of the battle, at least from the Scottish point of view. Admittedly both were written many years later. But Wyntoun tells us that his treatment of the reigns of David II and Robert II (1329–90) was closely based on a (now lost) anonymous chronicle; this probably dates from the 1390s, and although therefore not contemporaneous with Neville's Cross, could well have employed first-hand Scottish material (one participant in the battle who lived to 1390 was Robert Stewart – Robert II – himself; the anonymous chronicler may have been close to Robert).[22] As for Walter Bower, he too used the anonymous 1390s chronicle, but apparently independently of Wyntoun; and he provides some extra information which may have come from other fourteenth-century Scottish sources.[23] Wyntoun's and Bower's chronicles do seem to give a framework for working out what probably happened to the Scottish army in the battle, which in general is not inconsistent with what the English sources tell us. That said, it must be added that the result is my own speculation; as Prestwich stresses, we shall never be exactly sure about the course of events at Neville's Cross on 17 October 1346.

One thing on which most of the main sources agree, however, is that the day's first encounter took place some miles south of Durham, when William Douglas of Liddesdale, who was foraging with a force of perhaps around 500,[24] ran into the advancing English army at Ferryhill (five miles from Durham), and only escaped after suffering heavy casualties in a running fight that ended at Sunderland Bridge (three miles from Durham). There is also a general consensus that this took place very early in the morning. According to the *Lanercost Chronicle*, Douglas had gone foraging at dawn, which is not implausible; Wyntoun states that Douglas set out early,

---

[22]   Cf. S. Boardman, *The Early Stewart Kings: Robert II and Robert III* (East Linton, 1996), pp. 4–8, and 145–8. The first version of Wyntoun's chronicle (printed by Amours on the left-hand pages) finishes with the end of the anonymous chronicle in 1390, and may perhaps represent the actual anonymous text; in that case, the other two versions would give us Wyntoun's revision and extension of it.

[23]   For discussion of Bower's Scottish sources for this period, see *Scotichronicon*, ed. Watt, VII, xvii.

[24]   *Lanercost*, p. 348. Although Wyntoun states that Douglas took 'the mast part of thar gadering', a few lines later he says the foragers fled because 'thai were nocht of na mycht'; that is much more likely. He gives the total dead as 500 (the same number as he says died in the battle proper); that probably derives from a garbling of something like 'most of the foragers', and so would tally well with the *Lanercost Chronicle's* figure.

and also remarks on how early the English were ready; Bower says the English were moving at daybreak; and the Meaux chronicler seems to time the encounter at 'around the hour of prime [daybreak]'. The likelihood is that the English had set out before dawn, no doubt in order to catch the Scots before they could escape (Thomas Rokeby, for one, would have remembered the Scottish elusiveness on the 1327 Weardale campaign).[25] Since most of the English army was mounted, it could have covered the four miles from Bishop Auckland to Ferryhill quite quickly – and its vanguard could then have chased William Douglas back towards the Scottish encampment in Bearpark.[26]

The *Lanercost Chronicle* describes Douglas frantically shouting, 'David! rise quickly; look, all the English are attacking us.' Whether or not the king really was roused from his bed, there can be no doubt about the shock suffered by the Scots; as Wyntoun puts it, 'Oure ost than all effrayit was.' They had good reason to be afraid: they were not expecting to have to fight a serious battle, and would surely have remembered the slaughter at Dupplin and Halidon. There was a difference, however. At Dupplin the Scots had greatly outnumbered Edward Balliol's forces, and so had charged confidently, while at Halidon they were more cautious, but had to attack because they were trying to relieve Berwick; both times they were defeated by defensively positioned archers and men-at-arms.[27] But at Neville's Cross they did not need to attack. Instead, the Scots left the park (which presumably was unsuitable for fighting) and, according to the Meaux chronicler, 'positioned themselves in a fairly steep place to await the English'. The English army was 'about a quarter of a mile away', a distance that would have kept the Scots out of range of English arrows.

The armies seem to have spent the morning staring at each other. Prior Fossor's letter (Document a) states that 'from about the hour of terce [*c.* 8.30 a.m.] until nones [*c.* 2.00 p.m.] they remained there, banners flying ... with little ground between them', and that the battle eventually started at the hour of nones. Thomas Sampson's letter (Document b) also says that the battle began at nones, and went on until vespers [*c.* 5.00 p.m.]; while the

---

25   Rokeby's rise to prominence began when, as a young squire, he discovered the Scots in Weardale; see below, p. 51.
26   The English appear to have gone from Bishop Auckland to Merrington (*Lanercost Chronicle*, which locates the initial encounter there; also *Scotichronicon*), to Ferryhill (*Wyntoun*), to Sunderland Bridge (*Wyntoun, Scotichronicon*) and thence to Durham. The route Bishop Auckland–Merrington–Ferryhill is somewhat south of the direct Bishop Auckland–Durham line; perhaps, initially, a circuitous route was planned which would approach Durham from the south-east.
27   Nicholson, *Edward III and the Scots*, pp. 86–90, and 131–6.

ANDREW WYNTOUN'S *CHRONICLE*	*SCOTICHRONICON* BY WALTER BOWER	PRIOR FOSSOR'S LETTER	SAMPSON'S LETTER
	English manoeuvre from Auckland: to Merrington; to Sunderland Bridge		Archbishop of York moved from Auckland to Durham
Douglas foray in morning; met English at Ferryhill and Sunderland; defeated; 500 killed	Douglas foray in morning; met English at Ferryhill; defeated at Sunderland; 500 killed		
Scottish army arrayed in three divisions	Scottish army arrayed in three divisions	Hearing our men moving up to moor of Bearpark, Scots prepared to fight with battle lines drawn up	
		Armies remained in place from terce (9.00) to nones (2.00); banners flying; little ground between them	
While Scots preparing for battle, English archers fired on them	Formations approached the lines of battle	At nones (2.00) both sides fought	Battle fought from nones (2.00) to vespers (5.30)
John Graham attacked archers	John Graham attacked archers		
Moray's schiltrom; nearest to English: attacked at high dykes, was discomforted, and retreated	Moray's schiltrom attacked; fearful fight between ditches and hedges		Twice English archers and footsoldiers retreated
King's schiltrom was joined by remnant of Moray's; in very narrow place	King's schiltrom attacked by 10,000 archers + men-at-arms; David ensnared between ditches; captured.		Men-at-arms stood firm and fought stubbornly until archers and footsoldiers recovered
First two schiltroms retreated to join the third; together, suffered from archery and were defeated	Scots fled from the two whirlwind English attacks; Robert Stewart and earl of March saved themselves		
Flight took place over two miles. Final stand; Scots completely overcome; David captured		English won; David II was captured	Battle ended at vespers (5.30) with English victory
Scot casualties: 500, + 500 in foray, making 1000 in all	Scots casualties = 1,000		

Illustration 1: Comparative chart of the accounts of the battle given by original sources.

LANERCOST CHRONICLE	ANONIMALLE CHRONICLE	GEOFFREY LE BAKER	MEAUX CHRONICLE
	Morning: English confessed themselves; took Holy Communion	Archbishop of York etc. went to meet the Scots	Scots and English met between Durham and Bearpark at around the first hour (6.30)
Douglas foray at dawn, with 500 men. Met English at Merrington. Defeated; most of men killed	Douglas foray in morning (as *Lanercost Chronicle*)		That morning many Scots plunderers were killed
Douglas got David II out of bed	(as *Lanercost Chronicle*)		
Scottish army arrayed in three divisions	(as *Lanercost Chronicle*)		Both armies in three divisions; archers on flanks. Scots chose steep place, and awaited English; 1/4 mile between armies
At about third hour (9.00) English fell on the Scots near Durham. Archbishop of York blessed his men	Around terce (9.00) archbishop addressed English army and ordered them to fight vigorously		500 English archers showered Scots; made them leave chosen place and go forward to battle
		Scots withstood English arrows at beginning of the battle	
	Soon the ranks fought strongly; and two or three times rested by agreement and then fought again	Scots wearied from exertion and terrified by blows from axes	At first English retreated. Then when got strength back charged Scots. At length so tired that break needed
		Scots packed tightly together; when one fell ten fell with him; others then retreated	Both sides having regained strength, cruelly fought again
Robert Stewart and Earl of March fled	(as *Lanercost Chronicle*)	Earl of March fled	March and Stewart saw English prevail, and fled on horseback
English victory	Scots defeated around the hour of vespers (5.30)	Rest of army stood round David until barely 40 survived. David finally captured	David II wounded, and captured while fleeing
Nearly whole of Scottish army captured or killed		Rest killed or captured; fugitives pursued. Heavy Scottish casualties	

Anonimalle Chronicle relates that 'around the hour of terce' the Archbishop of York addressed the English army, and that the Scots were finally defeated 'around the hour of vespers'. These three sets of timings are consistent, and indicate that the English army (or at least the first part of it) took up its position near Neville's Cross (only a mile from the edge of Bearpark) at about nine o'clock, when the Archbishop of York made his speech, but that nothing then happened for another five hours.[28] A long wait was not unusual in medieval battles, especially when both sides wanted to stay on the defensive; Agincourt, where the English and French looked at each other for at least three hours, is one example.[29] The wait would also, of course, have provided time for the whole English army to be assembled – and perhaps rest after its early march. For the Scots, some of the time would have been spent in arranging the army into the usual three divisions: the first under John Randolph, earl of Moray, and William Douglas, who were probably the best Scottish commanders; the second under David II himself; and the third and largest under Robert Stewart and Patrick, earl of March.[30]

Whether or not the Scots now wanted to fight is unclear. The position they were in is not unlike that which their predecessors had taken in Weardale in 1327, when the stand-off between the Scottish and English armies lasted several days. But then, crucially, the River Wear divided the two armies, and so the English archers could be kept at a distance.[31] Unfortunately for the Scots, that was not the case at Neville's Cross. Instead, the battle apparently began in the early afternoon, when (according to the Meaux chronicler) 500 English archers advanced and started to fire on the Scots. This seems to be corroborated in Wyntoun's account, which narrates that 'And quhill thai were arrayand, [the morning's waiting-time is not mentioned] / The Inglis archeris come sa neirehand / That schute amang thaim weill mycht thai.' One Scottish response, by John Graham, earl of Menteith, was to beg to be allowed to charge the archers with 100 horsemen, which he claimed would scatter them (that is how Robert I had

---

[28] I assume that the Meaux chronicler's statement that the initial Scottish–English encounter 'at around the hour of prime', although said to have been between Durham and Bearpark, actually relates to the killing of the foragers, which the chronicler then mentions (Document e). Otherwise, only the *Lanercost Chronicle* (Document c) gives an early time ('about the third hour'); but like the *Anonimalle Chronicle* and Sampson, it makes the battle end at vespers. Since the *Anonimalle Chronicle* (which is closely related to the *Lanercost Chronicle*) gives the third hour as the time of the archbishop's speech, I suggest the *Lanercost Chronicle* confused that with the start of the actual fighting.

[29] C. Allmand, *Henry V* (London, 1992), p. 91.

[30] Sometimes known, especially in English sources, as Patrick, earl of Dunbar.

[31] Nicholson, *Edward III and the Scots*, pp. 31–2.

dealt with the English archers at Bannockburn): 'Sa sall we fecht mare sekirly'. But no-one would join him – 'for no-one dared to commit himself to such a risk', wrote Bower. So Graham charged on his own, managed to disrupt the archers temporarily, and then got back to the Scottish army, although at the end his horse was killed. The idea of one knight charging home might seem unlikely, but the English longbow was not in fact particularly accurate, and a single individual wearing good armour and mounted on a fast horse was probably difficult to bring down. From the Scottish point of view, therefore, it is a pity that Graham did not receive the cavalry support he wanted.

It is just possible that Graham may have been refused support not out of fear, but for tactical reasons. While the Meaux chronicler says that the English archery provoked the Scots into advancing from their position, Geoffrey le Baker (Document f) records that 'they withstood the arrows of the English at the beginning of the battle', because they sheltered with bent heads under their helmets and behind their shields. It would, of course, have been the well-armed men, presumably in the front ranks, who did that. Also, there may not have been very many English archers present. There certainly were 1,200 from Lancashire, but whether the 3,000 from Yorkshire recorded in Wodehouse's account roll were actually there is not absolutely clear. Perhaps significantly, le Baker states that there were a thousand archers from Lancashire, but does not mention the Yorkshire ones. Thus it may not have been the case that the Scots were forced into attack by massed volleys of English arrows. Instead, it may have been the reverse: that the archery did not damage them so much as they feared, and that therefore they came to believe that the battle could be won after all.

Whatever the effect of the archery, the Scots now started the main part of the battle by advancing to the attack. According to Wyntoun, the earl of Moray's schiltrom[32] came to blows first, but its formation was broken up by high dykes; it was 'discomfit sone', and its survivors then 'held thar way withoutin hone [stopping]' (or 'spede thaim ful tyte', in the chronicle's later versions) to the second schiltrom, which the king commanded. That, however, was in 'a rycht anoyus place' where the Scots had no room to fight, and so they could not resist their enemies. Therefore the remnants of

---

[32] Wyntoun actually uses the terms 'battall' (battallion), 'rout' (army), and (in the later versions) 'eschele' (division) rather than schiltrom. Strictly speaking, schiltrom (which according to the *Oxford English Dictionary* was more an English term than a Scots one) probably means a massed defensive formation; but I follow the looser modern practice of using it rather than the less vivid 'battallion' or 'division' simply to describe the separate blocks of the Scottish army. Note le Baker's stress on the Scots' use of shields against the initial archery attack.

both schiltroms finally joined with Stewart's division, which was waiting nearby and did have 'rovme to stand and fycht'. But there the English archers came into play again – 'for of arowis sic schot thare was / That feill were woundit in that place' – and so the first two schiltroms were defeated, while (as Bower puts it) Robert Stewart and the Earl of March 'followed wise advice and saved themselves with the help of an about turn'.

Various modern depictions of the battle show the three Scottish divisions arranged in a right-to-left formation straight across the battle area, but that can hardly be reconciled with Wyntoun's account (nor, indeed, with the likely width of the field). When first Moray's and then the king's divisions were repulsed, it is difficult to envisage sideways withdrawals; retreats normally go backwards! It certainly makes much more sense to locate the third division in the rear – and, indeed, both the *Anonimalle Chronicle* and Geoffrey le Baker call it the rearguard. Now Wyntoun states that the third division was by far the largest, and so the likelihood is that it was mostly composed of the mass of poorly-armed men;[33] these would have been kept in the rear, leaving the 2,000 well-armed Scots to bear the main brunt of the fighting. In that case, we may suppose that the first two schiltroms consisted of roughly 1,000 good troops apiece. They might, originally, have been arrayed side-by-side, but Moray's division probably marched forward first. Significantly, Wyntoun tells that 'The Erll of Murray and his menye / Wes neire than at the assemble' – that is, near the archers whom Graham charged.[34] But the Meaux chronicle states that English archers were on the flanks, and that a relatively small force opened fire at the beginning of the battle – presumably from only one flank. It is likely, therefore, that Moray's initial attack would have been towards that flank. It probably drove the archers back, but was then checked at the 'hie dykis', which must thus have been on one of the flanks: that seems to fit what Richard Lomas tells us about the fourteenth-century topography of the area.[35] The survivors of Moray's schiltrom would have fled backwards – but also, no doubt, away from the flank and thus towards the middle of the field. In that case, they would have come to King David's schiltrom (now standing obliquely behind them), and so were incorporated within it. But this combined force would surely not have attempted another attack in the area protected by the high dykes; instead, it can be envisaged as fighting either on the other flank, or, more probably, on the front of the English position. It was common English practice to station the main line across a

---

[33] Though not entirely; Wyntoun originally said that Stewart had 'mony gud men with him', though that was cut from the later versions of the chronicle.

[34] Or, perhaps, simply nearest to the English, i.e. forming the front rank; that would imply the three divisions were initially one behind the other.

[35] Below, pp. 65–76.

narrowing front (for instance at Dupplin, Crécy and Agincourt); at Neville's Cross that would correspond well both with the topography of the likely battlefield and with Wyntoun's description of how David's men were crushed tightly together. Moreover, his statement that the third Scottish division had much more room would make most sense if that division was furthest away from the English front. It would have been there, towards the rear of the original Scottish position, that the remnants of the first two schiltroms must eventually have found themselves trying to resist a full-scale English onslaught which was supported by massed archers, and where 'bathe the fyrste routtis rycht thare / At that assemble vincust ware.'

While this interpretation derives essentially from Wyntoun's chronicle, the English accounts also indicate a battle fought in stages. Thomas Sampson told his friends that 'twice our archers and soldiers retreated, but our men-at-arms stood firm and fought stubbornly until the archers and foot soldiers reassembled' (encouraged, according to the *Lanercost Chronicle*, by Henry Percy, who 'charged forth into the enemy's front line'). The Meaux chronicler records that initially the English were compelled to retreat, but when they had regained their strength, they charged the Scots: 'At last, because of their exhaustion and the length of the fight, they rested from the fight for a time, leaning on their spears and weapons', before the battle was resumed again. Similarly, the *Anonimalle Chronicle* says that both sides 'two or three times rested by agreement and then fought again'. No distinction between the Scottish schiltroms is made in the English sources, but the two retreats by the archers and footsoldiers would have been presumably when Moray's men and then King David's made their initial attacks; while the lulls in the fighting would most probably have come after these were driven back (that would fit the impression given by Wyntoun that the Scots had time to reorganise themselves). Le Baker describes the Scots as 'wearied from exertion, so terrified by the blows of axe-heads, yet standing, so that where perhaps there stood ten, each supporting the others, the felling of one with one blow meant the felling of all together'; that tallies with Wyntoun's stress on the cramped position in which David II's schiltrom found itself. And le Baker's reference to axes confirms what is implied in all the other accounts: that this was not so much a battle won at a distance by archery, but a close-quarter brutal slogging match.

For Abbot Bower, the Scots lost the battle when they fled before 'two whirlwind attacks so fiercely launched by the English'. Bower seems to conflate Wyntoun's three stages into two, but Scottish memories of 'whirlwind' English counter-attacks could well be accurate, especially with respect to what must have been a triumphant English advance after the first two Scottish divisions had fallen back on the third. And it was no doubt in the face of that advance and the accompanying archery that the third division turned tail – though probably not immediately, for the Meaux chronicler states 'at last many of the Scots fell', and only then did the flight take place. The cowardice of Robert Stewart and the Earl of March was mocked by English chroniclers, and has subsequently been criticised by historians;[36] while David II, for his part, probably never forgave them. Yet their flight is not entirely surprising: if the first two schiltroms of well-armed Scots had been unable to withstand the English, then could the crowd of poorly-armed men in the third have seriously been expected to change the tide of the battle? Moreover, the poorly-armed men would have been much more vulnerable to the archery recorded by Wyntoun than the men of the first two schiltroms.

For Robert Stewart, it must have been a case of *déjà vu*; thirteen years earlier, he had been at, and had escaped from, the Battle of Halidon.[37] But how could Stewart, March, and the men of their division flee so easily from Neville's Cross, when so many other Scots were captured? The obvious answer is, on horseback – as, indeed, the Meaux chronicler indicates. The third division, in the rear, was no doubt guarding the Scottish baggage and horses (both armies would have consisted largely of mounted infantry). But in that case, presumably, all the Scottish horses were either used in the flight or ran wild from the battlefield – and so the survivors of the first two schiltroms were abandoned to their fate. In the final stages of Bannockburn, Edward II's household troops had managed to get him on to a horse and out of the battle, so that he could escape to the safety of Dunbar Castle, where, ironically, he had been welcomed by the same Earl of March who now fled from Neville's Cross.[38] But David II could not be rescued like that, if the horses had gone. Instead, he and the rest of his army could only retreat on foot for 'twa myle and mare'. It is easy to imagine that tragic shambles of a retreat by the survivors of the first two Scottish schiltroms – being hounded by their pursuers and being picked off by English archery, until at last (in le Baker's words) 'they stood together like a round tower, protecting the king in the middle, until there were barely forty left surviving, of whom not one could flee away'. And so, finally,

---

[36] Interestingly, while Wyntoun recorded in the first version of his chronicle that Stewart and March escaped back to Scotland, he deleted this from the later versions; as Stephen Boardman has argued, he was very probably a Stewart sympathiser.

[37] Nicholson, *Edward III and the Scots*, p. 135.

[38] Barrow, *Robert Bruce*, pp. 229–31. March perhaps knew that, since he had served both Edward II and (in the 1330s) Edward III, if he was captured at Neville's Cross he was likely to be executed (as happened with the Earl of Menteith, and was threatened with the Earl of Fife).

King David himself, already wounded in the face by two arrows, was taken prisoner after his frantic hand-to-hand fight with John de Coupland.

David did at least survive the battle, and was joined in captivity by four earls, Douglas of Liddesdale, and at least a score of major barons. But many Scots were killed, including John Randolph, earl of Moray, Maurice Murray, earl of Strathearn, Sir Edward Keith, the marischal,[39] Sir David Hay, the constable, Thomas Charteris, the chancellor of Scotland, John Roxburgh, the chamberlain of Scotland, and numerous other Scottish barons and knights. These can all be added to the sad tally of Scottish mortality in the Wars of Independence: as can John Graham, earl of Menteith, who was executed for treason on Edward III's command because in the 1330s he had sworn allegiance to Edward (just as Walter Selby, the defender of Liddel, had been executed by David II at the beginning of the campaign).[40]

It was certainly a great English triumph. Yet it should be added that in the middle ages, few battles (Hastings apart) had absolutely decisive results. The other major English victories of the period – Dunbar, Falkirk, Dupplin and Halidon against the Scots, and Crécy and Poitiers against the French – did not bring permanent success in their wars as a whole. Nor, from the Scottish point of view, did Stirling Bridge or even Bannockburn. And nor, in 1346, did Neville's Cross. Indeed from the English point of view, as Prestwich concludes, the main significance is simply that it was not a defeat. Had the battle been lost, Edward III could hardly have continued the siege of Calais, and the post-Crécy euphoria would have collapsed; in those circumstances, would Edward have been able to conduct his subsequent campaigns in France? Also, an English defeat would have left the north of England defenceless before the Scottish army; who knows what David would have tried to do? In fact, of course, northern England was not left undefended. This was greatly to the credit of Edward III (who was one of the most thoughtful of all English kings) and his subordinates,

---

[39] Historians have generally followed the *Scots Peerage* statement (VI, 30–3) that Sir Robert Keith, commander of the Scots host at Bannockburn, was the marischal of Scotland who died at Neville's Cross; that identification is given, e.g., in *Scotichronicon*, ed. Watt, VII, 465. But Robert Keith must have died in the early 1340s, for his brother Edward had a royal charter of the marischal's office and lands in about 1345 (and certainly before the battle): *Registrum Magni Sigilli Regum Scotorum*, vol. I, *1306–1424*, ed. J. M. Thomson (Edinburgh, 1914), appendix II, no. 1027.

[40] Although a Northumbrian, Selby had been in the Scottish allegiance in and after 1318, but had gone back to the English side before 1327: *CDS*, III, nos. 610, 981, 1047, 1356. This explains why David II had him executed for treason, and solves the problem raised in M. H. Keen, *The Laws of War in the Late Middle Ages* (London, 1965), pp. 45–8.

especially the Archbishop of York; throughout the summer of 1346 they had kept the North in a most efficient and impressive state of readiness to deal with a Scottish invasion.

But what were the consequences for Scotland?[41] After the battle, naturally enough, southern Scotland was overrun by the English again – though not until 1347. The invasion was led by Edward Balliol, who was still recognised as King of Scots by Edward III. But now that David II was an English prisoner, that soon changed, because Edward realised that he could only benefit from David's capture by accepting that David Bruce, not Edward Balliol, was the Scottish king. That duly happened, and Edward Balliol was eventually abandoned by Edward III. So, ironically, one effect of Neville's Cross was finally to end the Bruce–Balliol conflict for the crown which started off the Anglo-Scottish wars in the first place.

A second consequence was that Scotland had to experience another eleven years without a king. It was run by the survivors of Neville's Cross, Robert Stewart and the Earl of March, together with the young Lord of Douglas, who had been a minor, and was abroad in 1346. These three came to dominate the top of the Scottish magnate class during David's captivity and beyond; most of the obvious balances to them had been killed or captured, and indeed several magnate families, most notably the Randolphs, had become extinct in the male line as a result of the battle. Thus Neville's Cross left a permanent mark on Scotland's political society.

Thirdly, although Robert Stewart in particular was in no hurry to bring David II home – certainly not on English terms – the king did have to be released eventually. Negotiations dragged on for years, and various English demands were rejected (including one, favoured by David, that a son of Edward III would succeed, rather than Robert Stewart, if David died childless). In the end – after an invasion of Lothian by Edward III and the French defeat at Poitiers – David was simply ransomed, in 1357, for 100,000 marks (£67,000), payable over ten years and guaranteed by twenty-three noble hostages. But the Scots were unable to finance the annual instalments, and so the issue of the ransom, the hostages, and relations with England became one of the determining features of Scottish politics for the following twelve years, until the outbreak of fresh Anglo-French warfare in 1369 relieved the pressure. And another determining feature, not surprisingly, is hostility between David II and

---

[41] The following four paragraphs derive from Grant, *Independence and Nationhood*, pp. 35–40 and 174–7. For fuller discussions, see: Campbell, 'England, Scotland and the Hundred Years War'; Nicholson, *Later Middle Ages*, ch. 7; A. A. M. Duncan, '*Honi soit qui mal y pense*: David II and Edward III, 1346–52', *Scottish Historical Review* 67 (1988), pp. 113–41; and Boardman, *Early Stewart Kings*, ch. 1.

Robert Stewart! The consequences of Neville's Cross were felt for a very long time in Scotland – just as David, himself, had to endure a piece of arrow-head embedded in his face until the mid-1360s.

For the main effect that Neville's Cross had on Scotland, however, I would look again to Edward III. My own opinion is that by the early 1340s he had already given up any notions of a serious take-over of Scotland. What he really wanted was a safe northern frontier, with a buffer zone of English-held territory in southern Scotland which would protect northern England from Scottish raids. He had previously tried to establish that in the 1330s, but had lost most of it by 1342. After Neville's Cross, however, the English hold of at least part of Scotland's southern shires proved much longer lasting. The Scots did whittle away at it in the 1350s, but it was largely regained in a short but devastating invasion in 1356. From then on, the Scots did not dare to antagonise Edward too much (he appears, indeed, to have bluffed them into keeping a truce). When David II died in 1371, a significant part of southern Scotland was still in English hands; and it stayed there until after Edward's own death in 1377.

Thus with Neville's Cross, the Anglo-Scottish conflict entered a new phase. It was no longer a war of conquest; it was about frightening Scotland, keeping a secure Border, and protecting the north of England from Scottish revenge. This was certainly achieved – as Prior Fossor, for one, appreciated, since he saw the battle as 'bringing to an end the pitiful discord which prevailed between English and Scots over the course of many years'. That was true enough, at least so far as northern England was concerned. After 1346 the conflict zone moved north of the Border, and following David's release in 1357 there was no more serious Scottish raiding until after Edward III's death. The Scots did not complete the recapture of the English-held buffer zone (apart from Berwick, Roxburgh and Jedburgh) until the 1380s, in the passage of war that led up to the Battle of Otterburn in 1388. From the Scottish point of view, it was that victory which marks the final end of the Wars of Independence, with Scotland, in the long run, having been successfully defended against English aggression.[42] Scotland, it should be remembered, won its wars against England in the later middle ages, despite catastrophic defeats like Neville's Cross. But, as Andrew of Wyntoun would surely have agreed, it would have been so much better for the Scots in the later fourteenth century had that invasion of England in 1346 never taken place.

---

[42] A. Grant, 'The Otterburn War from the Scottish Point of View', in *War and Border Societies in the Middle Ages*, ed. A. Goodman and A. Tuck (London, 1992), pp. 30–64.

John de Coupland – Hero to Villain

MARIE C. DIXON

Undeniably, the hero of the battle of Neville's Cross in 1346 was John de Coupland, an obscure Northumbrian squire. Not since 1174, when William the Lion was captured outside Alnwick, did the English have the same cause for celebration. The *Lanercost Chronicle*, after recounting the devastations committed by David Bruce as he moved south to Durham was, understandably, overjoyed at his defeat and lavished praise on his captor, thus

> John de Coupland dealt such blows among the enemy that it was said that those who felt the weight of his buffets were not fit to fight any longer.[1]

Being a shrewd Northumbrian, John de Coupland was well aware of the worth of his prize and would not hand him over to anyone other than the King of England. A grateful monarch rewarded him well, making him a banneret with an annuity of £500 for life. He was granted a further annuity of £100 for life for remaining with the king with his twenty men-at-arms. Of the annuity, £400 was to be paid from the customs from London, £100 from those of Berwick and the remaining £100 from those of Newcastle-upon-Tyne.[2] According to the Bank of England, who have a table of the values of the pound sterling from 1270 onwards, the value of one pound in 1350 would, in today's money, be £382.75. This would make the £600 granted to John de Coupland in 1346, worth £229,650 today.

John de Coupland was born, as far as can be ascertained, in Coupland in Northumberland, the son of John de Coupland. His uncle, Simon de Coupland, his father's elder brother, owned three parts of the manor of Coupland, together with Yeavering and Akeld.[3] Simon de Coupland died leaving an illegitimate daughter, Joan, who married Walter Mautalent. In 1337, Agnes, widow of William Mautalent brought an action of *novel disseisin* against John de Coupland.[4] The following year another action of

---

1   *Lanercost*, p. 351 (Document c). I am deeply indebted to Professor Michael Prestwich for reading this paper in draft form and for the supervision of my thesis of which it forms a part.
2   *CPR 1345–1348*, p. 226; *CDS*, III, 269.
3   *NCH*, XI, 214–18.
4   *CDS*, III, 227.

novel disseisin was brought against John by his cousin, Joan Mautalent, who was by this time a widow, in respect of a holding in Coupland, which consisted of 2 messuages and 14 acres of land.[5] Having the same surname, it seems very likely that the two widows, Agnes and Joan, were related through marriage. In 1339 the king ordered that the two actions of *novel disseisin* against John de Coupland were to be suspended as he was with the king in Flanders.[6] In 1340 John de Coupland brought a case against Joan Mautalent and, in defence of her charge of *novel disseisin*, stated that due to the irregularity of her birth, she could not inherit the estate of Simon de Coupland, and that he was the true heir of his uncle. The Court of the Bishop of Durham found that Joan was indeed illegitimate, and confirmed John as his uncle's heir.[7] That John was successful in disinheriting his cousin is confirmed by the Feudal Aids of 1346, as he paid 30*s*. for three parts of a knight's fee for three parts of the vills of Akeld, Yeavering and Coupland.[8] John de Coupland was married to Joan Strother, daughter of Henry Strother of Kirknewton and Moneylaws.[9]

---

[5] *CDS,* III, 234.

[6] *CDS,* III, 238.

[7] *Registrum palatinum Dunelmense: The Register of Richard de Kellawe, Lord Palatine and Bishop of Durham,* ed. T. D. Hardy (RS 62; 4 vols., London, 1873–8) III, 339–40.

[8] *Inquisitions and Assessments Relating to Feudal Aids: with other Analogous Documents Preserved in the Public Record Office, 1284–1431* (6 vols., London, 1899–1920), IV, 65.

[9] See Pedigree of Coupland in *NCH,* XI, 216. By drawing a distinction between Joan, the illegitimate daughter of Simon de Coupland and Joan, his heiress, Kenneth Vickers confuses the identity of the wife of John de Coupland. Joan, the heiress, he surmises was either a Strother or a Grey, but does not offer an explanation why Simon should leave Joan Strother or Joan Grey his estate. He left his estate to 'Joan, daughter of Alice, daughter of Simon, son of Margaret of Lanton'. As the maternal lineage of Joan is so clearly stated, and no mention is made of her father, it seems certain that Joan , the illegitimate daughter, and Joan, the heiress, was the same person. Also, if she was not, there would have been no reason for John de Coupland to have gone to the trouble of having her declared illegitimate in the bishop's court, and himself confirmed as the true heir. So, if Joan the heiress and Joan the daughter was the same person, who was Joan de Coupland? Madeleine Hope Dodds, writing in the *NCH,* XIV, 247, refers to the *NCH,* XI, 218 n, and states that Joan de Coupland was a Strother. She got the family right, but the wrong parents. To confuse the matter even further, Robert Surtees, in his *The History and Antiquities of the County Palatine of Durham,* IV, 137 n. (e), identifies her as the sister of Agnes, but does not hazard a surname. There is, in the Northumberland Record Office at Gosforth in the *NRO Catalogue A–16 Swinburne, 97, No. 4/41,* a receipt from Joan de Coupland to her brother

John de Coupland must have entered the king's service sometime before 1339, for in that year the king granted 'his valet', John de Coupland, an annuity of £20 for 'his long and faithful service'.[10] In 1340, he was at the castle of Wark-on-Tweed, when with Sir Thomas Gray and Sir Robert Manners, they discomforted the Earls of Mar and Sutherland returning to Dunbar with 2,000 beasts and many prisoners, relieving them of their plunder and sending them home empty-handed.[11] In 1344, he was termed a 'king's yeoman'.[12] After Neville's Cross he was constantly in the king's service, going overseas again in 1347.[13] From 1347 until his death he was Constable of Roxburgh Castle and Sheriff of Roxburghshire, although he was relieved of his command suddenly and frequently during his career.[14] He was custodian of Berwick-on-Tweed from 1357 to 1363, but again his tenure was interrupted, for he was dismissed from his post in June, 1362.[15]

On many occasions he served as conservator of truces and on other border commissions. He was escheator for the county of Northumberland in 1354 and 1356[16] and sheriff in 1350, 1351, 1353, 1354 and 1356.[17] As sheriff in 1351, 1352, 1353, and 1356, he had custody of David Bruce, who had been allowed to visit Scotland to negotiate a peace,[18] but on the last occasion in 1356, peremptory orders were given to have him removed and another put in his place.[19] These sudden dismissals were a frequent feature of his career but he was never openly disgraced. Although created a

---

Henry de Strother for 80 marks paid to her for the farm of the manor and barony of Wark-on-Tweed. It was issued in London on 27 April, 49 Ed.III, and bears her seal. A look at the pedigree of the Strothers of Kirknewton, *NCH*, XI, 132, shows Joan as the daughter of Henry Strother, and sister of Henry Strother. No other details of her are given, except that she was living in 1372, which is the year Joan de Coupland disposed of all her lands in Northumberland to the Earl of Arundel.

[10]   *CDS*, III, 238.
[11]   *CDS*, V, 269; *Scalacronica: The Reigns of Edward I, Edward II, and Edward III*, trans. H. E. Maxwell (Glasgow, 1907), p. 112.
[12]   *CCR 1343–1346*, p. 354.
[13]   *NCH*, XI, 219 n. 6.
[14]   *Calendar of the Fine Rolls Preserved in the Public Record Office* (22 vols, London, 1911–62), V, 494; *Rot. Scot.*, I, 692, 693, 714, 718, 740, 748, 756, 761, 777, 781, 858, 861, and 880.
[15]   *Rot. Scot.*, I, 801, 807, 841, 847, and 864.
[16]   *CPR 1354–58*, pp. 52 and 358.
[17]   PRO *Lists and Indexes* IX, Lists of Sheriffs, 97 (There is a note on page 96 stating that subsequent additions and amendments to the Northumberland list are based on the list of C. H. Hunter-Blair, 'The Sheriffs of Northumberland', *Archaeologia Aeliana*, 4th series, 20 (1942), pp. 24–89, and 21 (1943), pp. 3–46).
[18]   *Rot. Scot.*, I, 750–73.
[19]   *CPR 1354–1358*, p. 326.

banneret after Neville's Cross, remarkably he never took up knighthood, and in 1358, the king granted him exemption from knighthood for life.[20] In 1359 he was appointed Deputy Warden of the East March, along with Richard Tempest.[21] In the same year he made a nuncupative will at Wark-on-Tweed, when he was about to set out for some distant destination in the king's service.[22] It was while he was on the king's service, on 20 December, 1363, as he was crossing Bolton Moor, that he was attacked and killed.[23] Also killed with him were Nicholas Bagot, an attorney of Newcastle,[24] and William Kendale.[25]

It took three commissions of enquiry to arrive at the circumstances of the murder of John de Coupland. On 28 December, 1363, Henry Percy, Ralph Neville, Henry del Strother, Alan del Strother and Richard Horsley were appointed to enquire and arrest the murderers.[26] It was ascertained that the murderers were John de Clifford, his brother, Thomas, his servant Thomas Forster and others who were named, together with five unnamed pages. Nine were armed with lances and there were eleven archers. They had waited for John de Coupland and had killed him in a premeditated attack, but as far as the jurors knew, no one had hired them and no one had received them afterwards, as they had at once fled to Scotland.[27] Among those named, were Alan, Richard and William Vaux, kinsmen of John de Clifford whose mother had been Elizabeth Vaux. Henry de Lucker, another kinsman of John de Clifford, was also named. Constance de Lucker was the aunt of John de Clifford.[28]

The king was not satisfied with the findings of this enquiry, and on 20 January 1364 commissioned Aymer de Athol, William de Nessfield, Henry de Bellerby and Thomas de Brotby, to arrest the murderers and imprison them at Newcastle-upon-Tyne.[29] This enquiry revealed that John de Clifford and some of the others had fled to Ford, where William Heron had sheltered them in his castle. The record states that William Heron and

---

20 *CPR 1358–1361*, p. 121.

21 *Rot. Scot.*, I, 843.

22 *Wills and Inventories Illustrative of the History, Manners, Language, Statistics, etc., of the Northern Counties of England, from the Eleventh Century Downwards, Part i*, ed. J.· Raine (SS 2; 1835), pp. 29–30.

23 *CPR 1361–1364*, pp. 453–4.

24 A. Macdonald, 'Calendar of Deeds in the Laing Charters Relating to Northumberland', *Archaeologia Aeliana*, 4th series, 18 (1950), p. 117.

25 *CPR 1364–1367*, pp. 200, 217.

26 *CPR 1361–1364*, p. 453; *Calendar of Inquisitions Miscellaneous, Chancery, Preserved in the Public Record Office* (London, 1916–), *1348–1377*, p. 195.

27 *Calendar of Inquisitions Miscellaneous 1348–1377*, p. 195.

28 London, Public Record Office, Just 1: 661.

29 *CPR 1361–1364*, p. 454; London, Public Record Office, Just 1/661.

his sons, Richard Tempest, Nicholas Raymes and others were aiders and abettors of the felons.[30] The sheriff, unable to arrest the murderers, was then ordered to arrest those who had aided and abetted them, and they were ordered to appear before the king and his council at Westminster. At this point, thirty-five knights and squires appeared at the court in Newcastle and agreed to act as sureties for their appearance.[31] As a result of the proceedings at Westminster, William Heron was imprisoned in Bristol Castle, William Lilburn in Old Sarum Castle, William Heron (son) in Winchester Castle, John Heron in Oxford Castle and Roger Heron in Gloucester Castle. Joan, widow of Thomas Heton, was imprisoned in the Tower of London, as an aider and abettor.[32] They were released in 1366 after payments were made to the king.[33]

The third enquiry on 3 May 1364, had a different purpose. Gilbert de Umfraville and Aymer de Athol with others were to enquire into all felonies, trespasses, conspiracies etc., in the County of Northumberland.[34] The outcome of this enquiry was a pardon from the king, together with a fine of 1,000 marks to be levied on the men of Northumberland for all trespasses, felonies etc., excepting the death of John de Coupland and all other treasonable offences. The men of Newcastle were likewise pardoned for a fine of £200.[35]

The murderers were not caught, for they had fled the country. John de Clifford went to France where he joined the English army. Of the others there is no record of their activities. In 1366 Clifford's escheated lands were granted to Joan de Coupland.[36] In 1367 there was panic because of a rumour that Clifford was allegedly planning to capture Bamburgh Castle, but this appears to have been unfounded and sounds too far-fetched to be true. On 2 March 1377, at the special request of the nobles, magnates and the commonalty of the realm, John de Clifford was granted a pardon for the death of John de Coupland by the king in Parliament.[37] Henry de Lucker was tried and outlawed for his part in the murder, but in 1381, at the request of the Earl of Northumberland, he was pardoned.[38] The only unlucky person appears to have been Thomas Brewster, who was arrested and indicted, but insisted that he was not the Thomas Brewster involved in

---

[30] London, Public Record Office, Just 1/661.
[31] *Ibid.*
[32] *CCR 1364–1368*, pp. 84, 152.
[33] *CPR 1364–1367*, p. 338; *CCR 1364–1368*, pp. 265, 291: *CDS*, IV, p. 123.
[34] *CPR 1361–1364*, p. 539; London, Public Record Office, Just 1/661.
[35] *CPR 1364–1367*, p. 260.
[36] *CPR 1364–1367*, pp. 200, 217.
[37] *CPR 1374–1377*, p. 435.
[38] *CPR 1377–1381*, p. 591.

the murder. While his case was pending, he escaped, was re-captured, and there is reason to believe that he was eventually hanged.[39]

For John de Coupland to have been murdered by his own countrymen, men who were his neighbours and colleagues, suggests a motive of deep hatred or fear. There was nothing in the enquiries to suggest a possible motive for his death. The idea of robbery was soon dropped. That the murder was committed for nine horses and five mail-bags of jewels worth £200 was too risible to be true. There are, however, three possible motives, the most obvious being money. The second could have been the apparent favour of the king in respect of the granting of office, for John de Coupland held office many times, often more than one office at the same time. Or, thirdly, could it have been because of the lands and estates that John de Coupland was so busily acquiring, sometimes by very dubious methods?

It is difficult to see how money could have been the motive as the murderers could not hope to gain financially by his death. Resentment against his annuities must have been very strong, especially by those who faced debts and poverty as a result of the destruction of their lands, but killing him would not have improved their state. In fact, they stood to lose everything they owned, lands, possessions, and even their lives, if caught. Likewise, had office been the motive, it is unlikely that Coupland's killers would have been granted the positions he had held. If found responsible for John de Coupland's death, the murderers would have been disinherited, with their lands forfeited to their overlords. They could not conceivably then have gained his offices. It has been suggested that they were persuaded by others, for reasons of their own, to kill John de Coupland.[40] This seems unlikely in view of their status. John de Clifford was a landowner in his own right, holding Ellingham and Newstead from the king. Henry de Lucker also held lands in Northumberland of Henry Percy. The loss of lands, livelihood, status and position, was a high price to pay for doing someone else's dirty work. This was not a contract killing by faceless assassins.

There are many advantages to both the holding of office and the possession of land, but the greatest advantage of land over office is the fact that it is inheritable, whereas office is not. Although holding office was perhaps the best way impoverished landowners were able to augment an income diminished by the Scottish raids, they needed their estates to qualify for office. Tenure of office might be for a term as short as a year or two, and the Scottish raids, although frequent and devastating, were not

---

[39]   London, Public Record Office, KB 27/447 m.25d.
[40]   J. A. Tuck, 'Northumbrian Society in the Fourteenth Century', *Northern History* 6 (1971), pp. 36–8.

permanent, but land was a lasting, tangible, inheritable asset. The families who were able to hold on to their estates retained the hope of recovering their fortunes in the future when conditions improved. At a time when land conferred wealth, power, status and all the trappings that went with ownership, land did not become secondary to office; land was always of paramount importance.

A look at the acquisitions of land by John de Coupland, before and after Neville's Cross, reveals some very interesting facts about the character of the man, and goes a long way to explaining his unpopularity in the county. As we have already mentioned, as early as 1339 he had evicted two widows, Agnes Mautalent and his cousin, Joan Mautalent, from their homes, which can only be described as small-holdings. In 1340, he had his cousin declared illegitimate, so that he could inherit his uncle's estate. In 1344 he petitioned the king and was granted the lands of John Herring, William Rodom and Richard Edmanston in Alnwick, Little Haughton, Prendwyk, Reaveley, Ryal and Hetherslaw, which had escheated to the king because of their treason in the reign of Edward II.[41]

It is not known when the Couplands leased the castle of Wark-on-Tweed, but they were living there when Coupland made his will in 1359. Once established there, it did not take them long to start buying up land in and around the barony of Wark. In 1348, John de Coupland bought from Robert Archer a moiety of the manor of Mindrum. By 1362 he had acquired the rest of the manor from Sir John Strivelyn.[42] Also, in 1348, William, son of Sampson of West Newton, sold his lands in the town together with his wood 'Ruttock' and half the lordship of the town to Coupland.[43] It is not known how or when the Couplands acquired Presson, but in 1365 it belonged to Joan de Coupland.

About this time, in 1347–8, the king granted to John and Joan de Coupland, for their lives, the lands of William de Courcy in the counties of York, Cumberland, Westmorland and Lancaster, which had come into the king's hands by the death of William. This grant was in part satisfaction of the £500 annuity granted to him in 1346 for the capture of David Bruce. The difference was to be paid by the port of London, with the port of Newcastle paying the remaining £100.[44] This grant of lands, in addition to those they already held in Northumberland, made John and Joan de Coupland major landowners in the north of England.

---

[41] *CCR 1343–1346*, p. 354.
[42] F. W. Dendy, 'Extracts from the De Banco Rolls Relating to Northumberland', *Archaeologia Aeliana*, 3rd series, 6 (1910), pp. 52 and 56.
[43] Macdonald, 'Laing Charters', p. 115.
[44] *CPR 1345–1348*, p. 370.

John and his wife continued to buy more lands, particularly along the border with Scotland. In 1353, John Archer (son of Robert Archer) sold the manor of Kilham, which included the manor of Paston, to Coupland.[45] At the same time they bought a small-holding of 40 acres of land and 6 acres of meadow from Peter and Agnes Crabbe, these lands being Agnes's inheritance.[46] The above transactions suggest that the Archers, but certainly the Crabbes, were in financial difficulties. The purchase of the Crabbes' lands demonstrates all too clearly the plight and poverty to which the small landowners had been reduced. Also, in Paston and Shotton, the Couplands requested and were granted, the lands of John Trollop, escheated because John had joined the Middleton rebellion in 1317.[47]

In 1351/2, John de Coupland was involved in an acrimonious law suit with the Lilburns, the large Heron family, Thomas Heton, Henry de Lucker, and Thomas Gray over the Huntercombe moiety of the Muschamp barony. Nicholas Huntercombe sold his half of the Muschamp barony to John Lilburn, who in turn sold it to John de Coupland. This included tenements in Ford, Scremaston, Crookham, Barmoor, Ditchend, Ulcestre, Unthank, a moiety of the manor of Wooler, Hethpool and Heddon. With the lands, John Lilburn sold the services of his tenants. For some time before the Black Death, but certainly after, services due through land tenure had either lapsed or been commuted to a cash rent. In this case they must have lapsed, for when John de Coupland tried to enforce them, the tenants refused and he was forced to file a case in the Court of Common Pleas. The tenants were summoned to Westminster to state by what services they held their lands.[48] The Herons were the largest group of tenants, and in 1350, Sir William Heron had divested himself of the demesne of Ford to his son Roger, who was under age. Roger enfeoffed his younger brothers, Thomas and Robert, also under age. In the ensuing court case, Coupland maintained that the Herons were out to defraud him, and asked the court to force the brothers to assign the services due to him. Thomas and Robert said they would, if as minors they could legally do so. The court said they could, so they did, but when Coupland demanded that Roger should attorn also, the judges said they needed time to consider their decision.[49] This suggests that the judges were not entirely on the side of John de Coupland. Perhaps, this was the cause of the ill-feeling between the Herons and John de Coupland, and why they sheltered his murderers in 1363.

---

[45] Dendy, 'Extracts from De Banco Rolls', p. 54.
[46] *Ibid.*, p. 53.
[47] *CPR 1358–1361*, pp. 233–4.
[48] *CDS*, III, 284–5.
[49] London, Public Record Office, CP40/367, m. 78, 228d.

John de Coupland also owned land in Durham, for in 1360 Thomas Gray granted him half the manor of Crookhall. He immediately sold his moiety to William and Agnes Coxhow, who granted him a rent for Crookhall and Clifton in Tindale-gill. It seems likely from the above, that Crookhall must have been the security for a loan that Thomas Gray could not repay and thus he forfeited half the manor. The sale to William and Agnes must have been in the form of a mortgage, hence the payment of rent.[50]

John de Coupland's acquisition of half the vill of Byker in 1350 was not in pursuit of landed wealth, but the power which was inherent in the service by which the tenancy was held from the king. The manor of Byker was held by Robert Byker, who settled half the manor on himself and his heirs, and the other half on his wife and their heirs. Robert died in 1349, whereon Hugh, his brother and heir, sold his half to John de Coupland in 1350. John Byker, another brother of Robert and heir to the other half, had been involved in the Middleton rebellion, for which he had been pardoned and his property restored. He inherited the other half of the manor, but two-thirds was held by Robert's widow, Juliana, as her dower. John Byker sold his one-third, plus the reversion of Juliana's two-thirds, to John and Joan de Coupland in 1357.[51] John de Coupland was very probably interested in acquiring the manor of Byker because of the services by which it was held. Byker was held by serjeanty which involved, besides a rent of 40s., the service of (a) carrying the king's writs to barons between the Tyne and the Coquet, (b) guarding the beasts and chattels taken in distraint for debts owing to the king, which could only be sold with his permission, and (c) performing the office of coroner, if he was absent. The service was considered so important that the heir of Byker was never in the wardship of anyone 'except the sheriff of the king's castle'.[52] This service gave its owner a great deal of influence and power. It also gave him the opportunity for making a great deal of money by its openness to extortion and peculation. Certain services by their nature, lend themselves to abuse, and without actually accusing John de Coupland of corruption, his 'sudden and frequent dismissals' from office are suggestive of this interpretation.

With the ownership of the serjeanty of Byker came the responsibility for the chantry of St Lawrence. It had been founded by John Byker in 1278, who had endowed it with lands for its foundation. In 1378/9, a jury found that the ancestors of the lords of Byker had given lands and tenements to the value of £4 yearly for the up-keep of the chantry, but that Joan de

50 Surtees, IV, 137–8.
51 CPR 1354–1358, pp. 122, 541.
52 Calendar of Inquisitions Post Mortem, I, 129 (inquisition of 44 Henry III).

Coupland 'had done away' with the chantry.[53] As Joan de Coupland died in 1375, the chantry must have been 'done away with' after the death of John in 1363, and before her own, and the £4 yearly income must have been appropriated by her.

It is really from 1358 that the true character of John de Coupland emerges, following the arrival in Northumberland of William de Nessfield, a royal official, who had been appointed escheator north of Trent. It was the job of the escheator to take into the king's hands the lands belonging to those who had been charged with treason. In this case, the treason was purported to have been committed during the reign of Edward II, when most landowners only survived by co-operating with the Scots. The ill-fated rebellion of Gilbert de Middleton in 1317 had involved most of the knightly families in Northumberland. Now forty years later, those who had taken part were either dead or very old.

The first instance of John de Coupland using William Nessfield and the charge of treason to benefit himself was to secure a stronger title to the moiety of the manor of Wooler that he had purchased from John Lilburn. Sir Ralph Neville had been granted a lease for life of this moiety of Wooler by Nicholas Huntercombe[54] on condition that it would revert on his (Ralph Neville's) death to John Lilburn and his wife Constance, who had purchased it from Nicholas Huntercombe, as part of the Muschamp moiety. It is not known whether John de Coupland was aware of this entail when he purchased the moiety of the Muschamp barony from John Lilburn, but it must have come to light when John Lilburn died in 1355. However, John de Coupland must have felt that his title was not strong enough, for in 1358 he petitioned the king that although he had bought the moiety of Wooler from John Lilburn, it had been found by an inquisition taken by William Nessfield that John Lilburn had been an adherent of Gilbert de Middleton, and therefore the land should belong to the king, and requested a re-grant. The king re-granted him the three knight's fees together with the reversion of the moiety after the death of Ralph Neville.[55] This re-grant broke the entail to the Lilburns, and explains why Katherine Lilburn (his second wife) brought a case against Joan de Coupland for dower in Wooler.[56] In her defence, Joan de Coupland produced a quit-claim, which she alleged Katherine had made in 1355. The case was postponed and nothing more is known.

---

[53]   *Calendar of Inquisitions Miscellaneous 1377–1388*, IV, 49–51; J. Hodgson, *A History of Northumberland* (Newcastle-upon-Tyne, 1820), pt. ii, vol. II, 342.

[54]   *Calendar of Inquisitions Post Mortem*, XII, 136 ; *Percy Chartulary* ed. M. T. Martin (SS 117, 1909), p. 433; Hodgson, *A History of Northumberland* , pt. iii, vol. I, 82.

[55]   *CPR 1358–1361*, p. 121.

[56]   Dendy, 'Extracts from De Banco Rolls', p. 60.

This accusation of treason against John Lilburn, while enabling John de Coupland to benefit, brought trouble to the Lilburn family and caused the lands of William Lilburn, son and heir of John, and Katherine, widow of John, to be escheated in December 1359. Their lands were restored to them on the confirmation that the loyalty of John Lilburn had never wavered.[57] It is not surprising that William Lilburn, who had married Elizabeth, daughter of Sir William Heron of Ford, was involved with the Herons in aiding and abetting John de Coupland's murderers.

In the following year, John de Coupland petitioned for, and was granted, the lands taken into the king's hands by William Nessfield of those charged with being enemies of the king, and rebels. These lands were in Hebburn, Howtel, Shotton and Paston and belonged to William Bentley, Nicholas de Hebburn and Roger Howtel. Also requested were the lands of Ellen Panbury in Howtel, Roger Wyderyngton in Shotton, John Trollop in Shotton and Paston, because they were traitors to the Crown and adherents of the Scots.

John de Coupland was not above taking lands from the Church. In the second half of the twelfth century, the monks of Kelso had been granted the 'grange called Colphinhope', which included the rights of pasture for 20 oxen, 20 cows and their calves and 200 sheep of the second year. During the Anglo-Scottish wars, this property had been escheated to the Crown and in 1359 it was petitioned for and granted to John de Coupland.[58]

The manipulations of the next case are rather convoluted, but they demonstrate that there was a degree of collusion between John de Coupland and William Nessfield. Henry Prendergast, a Scot with lands in Northumberland, joined the Scots before 1316, but in 1329 the lands which he had forfeited were restored to him under the terms of 'The Shameful Peace' of 1328. His lands included the fourth part of the manor of Akeld, which included Yeavering.[59] In 1335 another member of the Prendergast family, Adam, also joined the Scots, and his forfeited lands were granted to Thomas Heton. By the end of the year he was received into the king's peace and all his lands were restored. This cancelled the previous grant to Thomas Heton.

In 1359, the escheator, William Nessfield, reported that he had not taken into the king's hands the lands belonging to Adam Prendergast (previously granted to Thomas Heton), but that he had taken the lands of Henry Prendergast, which included the fourth part of Akeld. His reason for doing so was that Henry had lately (before 1316 and this was 1359) adhered to the Scots. He also claimed that the fourth part of Akeld had, at

57   CPR 1358–1361, p. 141.
58   CPR 1358–1361, pp. 233–4.
59   CPR 1327–1330, p. 522.

an earlier date, been the property of John de Coupland.[60] Hence, Adam continued to hold his lands while Henry suffered forfeiture. The claim that John de Coupland had once held the fourth part of Akeld was unsubstantiated. In spite of this, John de Coupland was granted the lands of Henry Prendergast, together with the fourth part of the manor of Akeld.[61] As mentioned above, Coupland had acquired the three parts of Akeld by disinheriting his cousin in 1340; now he had acquired the fourth part by escheat, giving him the whole manor of Akeld and Yeavering. Clearly, John de Coupland had many ways of acquiring lands. The losers were Henry Prendergast and Thomas Heton.

From the number of escheated lands that John de Coupland petitioned for and was granted, it soon becomes obvious that he must have been the one making the accusations. He had discovered a way to obtain the lands he wanted without paying for them, and it did not matter whether the owners wanted to sell. All he paid was the fine levied by the king for the grant. Nessfield was not a Northumbrian, and had spent most of his life at court and, therefore, would not have known which families had been involved with Gilbert de Middleton in 1317. The real losers were the landowners whose lands were escheated. They were paid nothing, and they had no redress at law as they could not sue the king, and they had the humiliation of seeing their lands granted to someone who clearly had no need of them. William Nessfield made a considerable number of escheats, and in most cases the lands were restored to their owners on payment of a fine, but from the number and location of the lands granted to Coupland, it was clear that he was using the Nessfield escheats to build and consolidate his position along the Anglo-Scottish border (ill. 2).

To return to his murder and his murderer, John de Clifford, it is curious that he was the only one to be charged with treason as well as murder. He was accused of (a) being an enemy of the king and a rebel, (b) riding at war in the realm, (c) killing John de Coupland, and (d) adhering to the Scots.[62] Apart from the charge of murder, the accusations read exactly the same as a Nessfield escheat. This raises the question, was John de Clifford aware that John de Coupland wanted his lands, and did he kill him to prevent him getting them, or was it in revenge because Coupland had already pointed the accusing finger at him? It would appear from the wording that the charges of treason had been prepared prior to Coupland's murder, and the charge of murder was then added to the other accusations. Furthermore, after the death of John de Coupland, the accusations of treason against the murderer were not only unusual, they were also

---

[60]   CDS, IV, 9.
[61]   CPR 1358–1361, pp. 233–4.
[62]   CPR 1364–1367, p. 200.

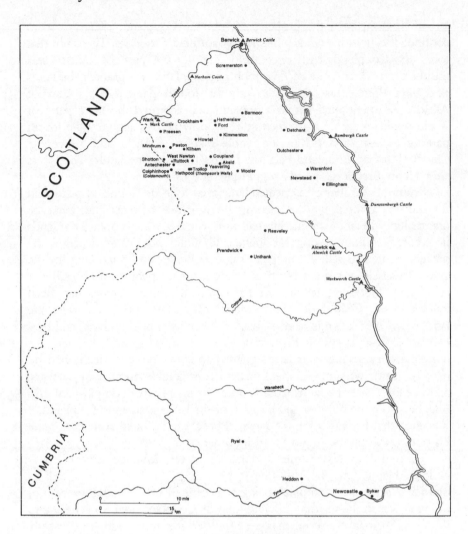

Illustration 2: Map of places connected with John de Coupland.

unnecessary. As John de Clifford held his lands of the king, this meant that as he had committed a felony, his lands automatically reverted to the king as his overlord without recourse to the charges of treason. Killing John de Coupland was the only way the local landowners had of stopping him taking their lands. It is not surprising that the lands of John de Clifford were granted to Joan de Coupland. Had they already been requested? It is significant that this type of escheat, based on treason charges, stopped after the death of John de Coupland.

Perhaps the most damning evidence of the greed and ruthlessness of John de Coupland was demonstrated in connection with the nuns of St Bartholomew in Byker. A dispute over a piece of land revealed the following:

> The jury find that at the feast of St Michael in 1361, the convent was almost desolate, by reason of the pestilence and the death of Isabel the prioress and the other nuns so that there were only two nuns left, Anne and Emma, who were about fourteen years of age, and to them came a certain nun of Lambley Priory called Margery, whom William calls prioress. By the consent of the two nuns and the convent of Lambley, she took charge of the house. In 1362/3 John de Coupland, then lord of the vill of Byker, exacted from the nuns a lease for 100 years at 40s. a year, and because he was a man of great power in the county, they dared not refuse him. The land was really worth 60s.[63]

A lease of 100 years was only useful to John de Coupland as something to sell. At a reduced rent of 40s. instead of 60s., he could have obtained a good price for it. The convent was the loser. They stood to lose 20s. a year for a 100 years, a sum which represented a third of their income. The Couplands were childless. The £600 annuity was granted to both for life, so Joan was well provided for and did not need the 20s., which, because of their poverty, the nuns so desperately needed. Was the murder of John de Coupland poetic justice?

---

[63]   *NCH*, XIII, 273.

Thomas Rokeby, Sheriff of Yorkshire, the Custodian of David II

ROBIN FRAME

My subject is one of the lesser figures – lesser, that is, than Ralph Neville or Henry Percy – who participated in the English victory at Neville's Cross. Lesser figures are often interesting in themselves, and their story can of course shed light on major matters. It is in that belief that I wish to introduce Thomas Rokeby. Those who live locally may have noticed a large Victorian house called 'Rokeby Villa' at the corner of St John's Road and Percy Terrace, close to the cross at Neville's Cross. The memory of Thomas Rokeby, or his family, is also preserved in Rokeby Square at Merry Oaks.

In 1346 Thomas Rokeby was sheriff of Yorkshire, and was one of the leaders of the Yorkshire force at the battle. We know very little about what he actually did at Neville's Cross. But two closely related northern chronicles, probably developed from the same Franciscan original, mention his presence. The *Anonimalle Chronicle*, associated with York, says that he was one of the commanders of the second 'battle' or battalion; it also places his nephew, another Thomas Rokeby, in the first battalion, led by Neville and Percy themselves. The Cumbrian *Lanercost Chronicle* is more forthcoming:

> Thomas de Rokeby, like a noble leader, gave the Scots such a cup that after they had sampled it once they did not wish to taste it again; and in this way he was an example to all who saw him fight bravely for the pious cause of his country.[1]

It is not very much. But there can be no doubt of Rokeby's importance, or of the trust Edward III placed in him. After the battle the captured King David was taken to York. On 8 December 1346, Rokeby was ordered to escort him from there to the Tower of London, together with two other Scottish noble prisoners. By 2 January 1347, what must have been a chilly winter journey had been made: the constable of the Tower issued a formal receipt confirming that David had been safely delivered into his keeping. Well before this the king had recognized Rokeby's services at Neville's Cross. At Calais on 12 November 1346, when news of the battle was still fresh, Edward granted him an annuity of 200 marks (£133 6s. 8d.), a large

---

[1] *Lanercost*, p. 351 (Document c).

sum by fourteenth-century standards, to be received from the revenues of
Yorkshire until it could be turned into lands in Scotland or elsewhere. The
last proviso is a reminder that in the months after the battle the English
seemed poised to overrun the Scottish lowlands, as they had done during
the 1290s and again in the mid-1330s; and indeed in May 1347 Rokeby was
one of the leaders of a force that went with Edward Balliol from Carlisle 'to
recover the kingdom of Scotland which belonged to him by right of
inheritance'.[2] This new wealth marked Rokeby's military and social
promotion by the king into the élite group of knights-banneret, who were
expected to have an income several times larger than that of an ordinary
knight.

So who was Thomas Rokeby? What does his career tell us about the
impact of the Anglo-Scottish wars on the prospects of able and ambitious
northerners? To what extent did Neville's Cross open further doors for
him?

Thomas Rokeby was a Yorkshireman, but he was very close indeed to
being a Durham man. For at least a century and a half his family had held
lands at Rokeby (the modern Rokeby Park), which lies at the northernmost
extremity of the North Riding, just across the Tees from Barnard Castle.
They were not particularly rich, nor is it certain that Thomas himself was
the eldest son. But the family estate, lying at the confluence of the Greta
and the Tees, was to be made famous – or moderately so – as the setting of
the long narrative poem *Rokeby*, which was published by Sir Walter Scott in
1813. The poem deals with imaginary events after the Civil War battle of
Marston Moor in 1644; it is full of topographical detail which Scott
carefully assembled during visits to Teesdale. At one point he has the
villainous Bertram Risingham riding out from Barnard Castle:

> Stern Bertram shunned the nearer way,
> Through Rokeby's park and chase that lay,
> And, skirting high the valley's ridge,
> They crossed by Greta's ancient bridge,
> Descending where her waters wind
> Free for a space and unconfined,
> As, 'scaped from Brignal's dark wood glen,
> She seeks wild Mortham's deeper den.[3]

Rokeby, Mortham and Brignall: these were the core properties that Thomas
Rokeby possessed, either by inheritance or by purchase, before 1346. By

---

[2]   H. S. Offler, 'A Note on the Northern Franciscan Chronicle', *Nottingham
Medieval Studies* 28 (1984), p. 58 (repr. H. S. Offler, *North of the Tees*, ed. A. J.
Piper and A. I. Doyle (Aldershot, 1996), ch. XV); *The Anonimalle Chronicle
1333–1381*, ed. V. H. Galbraith (Manchester, 1927), p. 27.

[3]   *Rokeby, a Poem, by Walter Scott, Esq.*, 4th edn (Edinburgh, 1813), II, v.

that date he had also acquired other lands and income, including property across the fells (in modern terms along the A66) near Kirkby Stephen in Westmorland, and an annual sum from Langbaurgh in Cleveland.

To understand how he had reached this position we must go back in time to 1327, and to a far less glorious military episode for the English. This was the year that the adolescent Edward III had come to the throne after the deposition of his father. Robert Bruce was still alive. He took advantage of the English political crisis to send an army across the border. The Scots crossed the Tyne and then the Tees. The English forces mustered at Durham. Assuming the Scots would retreat, they rode to the Tyne to cut them off. But the Scots did not appear, and the English came back southwards to Blanchland, searching for the enemy. In this confusion Edward proclaimed that whoever located the Scots would be knighted and rewarded with lands worth £100 a year. What happened next is recorded in the *Scalacronica*, written a generation later by the northern knight Sir Thomas Grey of Heton: 'Thomas de Rokeby brought the news that they were all at Stanhope . . . ; he earned the reward and became a knight'.[4] A more romanticized account is given by the Flemish writer Jean le Bel, who was present on the English side among a band of mercenaries from Hainault. Le Bel records the king's proclamation, and then tells of a young squire who approached the English lines and declared that he had located the Scots, finding them equally puzzled about the whereabouts of the English. He had been captured but released on condition that he at once reported to Edward that the Scots were eager for battle. Le Bel continues, 'and [the king] immediately gave that squire the £100 that had been promised, and knighted him in the presence of us all'.[5] (In fact the unchivalrous Scots left their camp-fires burning to fool the English, and slipped away north in the night.)

The traditional lack of emphasis on Rokeby's role at Neville's Cross may spring from the fact that in recounting this story Jean le Bel left the 'young squire' anonymous. When later in the century Froissart came to compose his far more famous chronicles of war and chivalry, for the early period he mostly copied from le Bel. As we have seen, Froissart's account of Neville's Cross, though almost wholly fictional, did a great deal to form the image of the battle and establish its heroes in the minds of later generations.[6] He records the names of the real or imagined leaders, but omits Rokeby. Had he known Rokeby's name from le Bel's account of the campaign of 1327, perhaps things would have been different; the newly

---

4   *Scalacronica, by Sir Thomas Grey of Heton, Knight*, ed. J. Stevenson (Maitland Club; Edinburgh, 1836), p. 154.

5   *Jean le Bel*, I, 61–4.

6   Above, p. 9.

knighted Sir Thomas might have shared in this fourteenth-century equivalent of tabloid fame.

That is a diversion from the main story. The point is that in 1327 Rokeby caught the eye of the new king, was knighted in the field, and received the first of the many rewards that helped to make his fortune. These were to include government office as well as cash and land. By 1335 he was sheriff of Yorkshire, a position which he held for two years and was to occupy again continuously from 1342 to 1349. The sheriff's role included the crucial task of mobilizing the men and resources of the largest shire in England for war against the Scots. In between his spells as sheriff he had another important job. He served as keeper of the castles of Edinburgh and Stirling and their hinterlands: he was in effect an English *gauleiter* in the dying days of what has recently been described as the 'Quisling' or 'Vichy' regime that Edward III was maintaining in southern Scotland.[7]

This outline of Thomas Rokeby's career before 1346 prompts several thoughts. Historians rightly emphasize the harmful effects recurrent warfare had on the prosperity of southern Scotland and northern England in the fourteenth century. But for some powerful individuals the picture was more rosy. This is familiar when we consider the topmost level of society. Politically and financially the Percies and Nevilles in England, and the Douglases in Scotland, did very well from the circumstances that compelled kings to rely upon and reward them. Rokeby is a good example of somebody further down the social scale who seized the opportunity to build a career more quickly and decisively than might have been possible in times of peace. He also, in a smaller way than the Percies and Nevilles, enhanced the standing of his family. There is an unexpected testimony to his success more than two centuries later. In 1593 Ralph Rokeby, a member of Queen Elizabeth's Council of the North, was to write a short family history to edify his young nephews. With that sort of moral confidence which today's older generation has so sadly lost, Ralph urged them 'to please and delight your selves in well-doing and also be affrighted with Infamy of vicious Lewd and foul Behaviour, to fear and Abhorr Shame and Dishonour as the Gates of Hell'.[8] And he picked out the deeds of the fourteenth-century Sir Thomas Rokeby as a model for the boys to follow, describing him as 'this Arch Peer of our Family'.[9]

---

[7] B. Webster, 'Scotland without a King, 1329–1341', in *Medieval Scotland: Crown, Lordship and Community. Essays presented to G.W.S. Barrow*, ed. A. Grant and K. J. Stringer (Edinburgh, 1993), pp. 223–38, at 227.

[8] *Œconomia Rokebiorum, an Account of the Family of Rokeby, written by Ralph Rokeby*, ed. A. W. C. Hallen (Edinburgh, 1887), p. 5.

[9] *Ibid.*, p. 11.

There is a second aspect of Thomas Rokeby's earlier career which is vital to an understanding of his role at and after Neville's Cross. As we have seen, he had impressed the king and had received many direct benefits from him. But his rise was also assisted by close relations with the really big powers of the region. In 1331, in what appears to have been his only continental excursion, he was among Henry Percy's suite on a diplomatic mission to France. In 1343 he witnessed a grant which Ralph Neville made to the church of Staindrop, close by the great Neville fortress at Raby. A year later he was again a witness, to a property-settlement made on the occasion of the marriage of Ralph Neville's son to Henry Percy's daughter. These associations provide a context for his military links with the two great lords, which emerge strongly in the years before Neville's Cross, when they served together as arrayers of troops, searchers for Scottish spies, and on other commissions. Rokeby was fully part of a key group of northern leaders whom Edward III trusted. The familiarity of those leaders with one another helps to explain the successful handling of the crisis of 1346 when it came during the king's absence. Moreover it may be significant that Rokeby's ties ranged northwards from Yorkshire. As well as being connected with the Nevilles, he sponsored candidates for ordination at Durham Cathedral. In 1346 co-operation with the forces of the Palatinate must have come more naturally to him than it would have done to a sheriff whose origins lay in a different region of Yorkshire.

In Thomas Rokeby we have a man whose life was shaped by the Anglo-Scottish wars; with hindsight we might almost see his whole career as a sort of preparation for Neville's Cross. As I have shown, his position was further advanced as a result of the battle. The English victory did not mean that the North suddenly passed from a state of war to one of peace. But it is true to say that for a time the region was more peaceful than it had been for several decades. The conditions that had carried Rokeby to prominence had altered. Was his career to end in a long diminuendo as an administrator in Yorkshire, or might Edward III find a further use for him? Although Rokeby had been knighted and then made a banneret by Edward, he had never been a member of the king's own military household, let alone a courtier; virtually his entire career had been spent in the provinces. Nor does he seem to have played any part in the French wars to which Edward had devoted most of his energies since 1338: the king, aware of the history of alliances between France and Scotland, sensibly tended to leave the northern gentry at home. There was, however, one other part of Edward's dominions where the experience Rokeby had gained as a soldier and administrator was in demand. That was Ireland, where royal authority and the English settlements made during the late twelfth and early thirteenth centuries were threatened both by a native recovery and by the unruliness of the settler aristocracy. Towards the end of 1349 Rokeby surrendered the office of sheriff of Yorkshire and was appointed governor of Ireland. He was to remain there almost continuously during the remaining eight years of his life, picking up further property which was sufficiently attractive to encourage the younger Thomas Rokeby to try to recover it after his uncle's death by serving in Ireland in the 1360s and 1370s with Lionel of Clarence and later governors. Sir Thomas himself found the demands of Irish warfare less easy to cope with than those he had experienced in the north of England. In Ireland he was not opposed to a clear-cut enemy such as the Scots; instead he had to conduct ceaseless local campaigns and diplomatic missions to try to pacify the splintered and competitive kins who inhabited the upland and wooded areas. In 1354, rather like a modern English politician marooned in Belfast, he was fruitlessly to plead with Edward III to let him come home from what he called 'this foreign land'.[10] The king turned a deaf ear to his plea; and Rokeby died suddenly, in the midst of arranging a military campaign in the Wicklow hills, in 1357. The date was 23 April, St George's Day, which somehow seems appropriate. Ironically, Sir Walter Scott, who may have known little or nothing about our Thomas Rokeby, was to give his imaginary seventeenth-century Rokeby an Irish dimension. Not only does he have him captured in his youth at the Battle of Yellow Ford (1598) when serving with Marshal Bagenal in Elizabeth's Irish wars, he equips him with a Gaelic Irish noble boy as his page. That lad, Redmond O'Neill, turns out to be the hero of the poem, and indeed marries Rokeby's daughter and heiress. The fourteenth-century Sir Thomas, who had no high opinion of the native Irish, might not have been amused.

Thomas Rokeby's role at Neville's Cross added to a reputation he had already won in the Anglo-Scottish wars, and led on to bigger things. Here we have somebody who began as a relatively insignificant squire from the Yorkshire–Durham border; went on to occupy high office in Yorkshire and in occupied Scotland; worked alongside the leading lords of the north; played a significant part in a stunning victory; escorted the King of Scots from York to London; and ended up as the king's representative at Dublin, presiding in Edward III's name at sessions of the Irish parliament and exercising authority over the greatest in the land. It is a tale of self-advancement, of a particular fourteenth-century kind: Thomas Rokeby may or may not have been hard-faced, but there is no doubt that he did very nicely out of the war. It would certainly be a mistake to present him as a model of respectability: he clashed violently with the Scropes over the possession of Brignall, and after his death his gains in Ireland were to be

[10] *Documents on the Affairs of Ireland before the King's Council*, ed. G. O. Sayles (Dublin, 1979), p. 207.

denounced as breaching a royal ordinance that forbade ministers to acquire property during their terms of office. Nevertheless, compared to a John de Coupland, he does seem to exemplify steady service, appropriately rewarded: the acceptable face of upward mobility. It is striking that an Anglo-Irish annalist writing at Dublin, who normally loses no opportunity to criticize English governors for unpaid debts and insensitive treatment of the locals, should express approval of Rokeby and attribute to him the saying, 'I prefer to eat and drink only from wooden vessels, and to spend gold and silver on supplies, clothing and soldiers' wages'.[11]

Further Reading
There is a brief outline of Rokeby's career, by C. L. Kingsford, in *Dictionary of National Biography* (Oxford, 1921–2), XVII, 152–3. For a fuller account, see Robin Frame, 'Thomas Rokeby, Sheriff of Yorkshire, Justiciar of Ireland', *Peritia* 10 (1996), pp. 374–96, which contains detailed references to the record sources on which parts of the present paper are based. There is further information on his Irish activities in A. J. Otway-Ruthven, 'Ireland in the 1350s: Sir Thomas de Rokeby and his Successors', *Journal of the Royal Society of Antiquaries of Ireland* 97 (1967), pp. 47–59. On the Rokeby family and lands, see *Victoria History of the Counties of England: Yorkshire North Riding*, vol. 1 (London, 1914), pp. 49–50 and 109–12. The campaign of 1327 is discussed in R. Nicholson, *Edward III and the Scots: The Formative Years of a Military Career, 1327–1335* (Oxford, 1965), ch. 3. On northern families and 'upward mobility', see J. A. Tuck, 'The Emergence of a Northern Nobility, 1250–1400', *Northern History* 22 (1986), pp. 1–17; and H. S. Offler, 'Murder on Framwellgate Bridge', *Archaeologia Aeliana*, 5th. series, 16 (1988), pp. 193–211 (repr. H. S. Offler, *North of the Tees*, ed. A. J. Piper and A. I. Doyle (Aldershot, 1996), ch. XIV). For the composition and convoluted plot of Scott's *Rokeby*, and for Scott's visits to Teesdale, see Edgar Johnson, *Sir Walter Scott: The Great Unknown* (2 vols., London, 1970), I, 384, 400–1, and 469–76. The Irish aspect of the poem is explored in G. A. Hayes-McCoy, 'Sir Walter Scott and Ireland', *Historical Studies X: Papers read before the Eleventh Irish Conference of Historians*, ed. G. A. Hayes-McCoy (Galway, 1976), pp. 91–108, at 92–96.

---

[11]   *Chartularies of St Mary's Abbey, Dublin*, ed. J. T. Gilbert (RS 80; 2 vols., London, 1884–6), II, 392–3.

Spoils of War? Durham Cathedral and the Black Rood of Scotland [1]

LYNDA ROLLASON

The victory at the Battle of Neville's Cross was a decisive one which, resulting in the capture of David Bruce and the failure of Franco-Scottish plans, both enabled Edward III to continue his offensive against France and relieved the north of England from further threat of Scottish attacks. It could be expected that such a notable victory would be followed by services of thanksgiving and other celebrations. The chronicler Knighton tells us that when King David was brought to London and lodged in the Tower Edward organised a 'triumph' to show off his prisoner. David, riding a large black charger so that he could be seen by the crowds, was led through the streets of the city as part of a procession which included a large number of armed men and representatives of the crafts in their liveries.[2]

There is no contemporary evidence that any service of thanksgiving took place in the cathedral at Durham, but later local tradition suggests that one was held and that it included gifts to the shrine of St Cuthbert. The evidence comes from the *Rites of Durham*, a text first written in 1593, which describes the furniture, decorations and ceremonies of the church of Durham on the eve of the Reformation. According to this source, the feretory of the cathedral was decorated for the occasion with the banners of the King of Scots, of Lord Neville and those of other noblemen. Which banners, says the *Rites*,

> were all brought to St Cuthberts Feretorie, and there the said Lord Nevell, after ye battel done in moste solemne and humble manner, did make his petition to God and that holy man St Cuthbert to accept his offeringe and did offer the aforesaid Jewells and Banners and ye holy rood crosse which was taken on ye Kinge of Scotts, to the Shrine of that holy and blessed man St Cuthbert within the Feretorie.[3]

1   This paper diverges quite considerably from that delivered at the conference. New pieces of evidence came to light as I worked up the notes. I must thank Mr Martin Snape for alerting me to the evidence for the possibility that the Black Rood was not captured at Neville's Cross.

2   *Knighton's Chronicle 1337–1396*, ed. and trans. G. H. Martin (Oxford Medieval Texts; Oxford, 1995), pp. 75–7.

3   *The Rites of Durham, being a Description or Brief Declaration of All the Ancient*

Local tradition is not necessarily to be relied upon but it is likely that a thank-offering would have been made at the shrine of so prominent a local saint, and reasonable also that the great victory that had been won on his very doorstep, so to speak, should have been attributed to his intervention. As the *Lanercost Chronicle* has it,

> Praise be to the Most High! victory on that day was with the English. And thus through the prayers of the blessed virgin St Mary and St Cuthbert, confessor of Christ, David and the flower of Scotland fell, by the just award of God, into the pit they had dug themselves.[4]

What is of particular interest in the *Rites* account of the gifts to the shrine of St Cuthbert is the specific mention of the donation of the Black Rood of Scotland, said to have been taken on David at his capture. This Black Rood was a reliquary in the shape of a cross, containing a portion of the True Cross, which had been a personal possession of St Margaret, queen of Scotland, who died in 1093, and who was venerated as a saint in the middle ages. This cross, according to her biographer, Aelred of Rievaulx, she held in her hands before she died and left 'as an heirloom to her sons'. It would seem that the Rood had assumed something of the status of a national symbol in the twelfth century when Aelred wrote, for he adds, 'That sacred cross called the Black Rood was, on account of their reverence for its sanctity, to all the Scottish people no less awe-inspiring than lovely.'[5]

That this relic had the status of a symbol of Scotland and Scottish identity is reinforced by its prominence in the early stages of the Anglo-Scottish conflict. It is noticed as being among the papers and relics in Edinburgh Castle examined by Edward I's commissioners in 1291.[6] But, more importantly, it was appropriated by Edward together with the Scottish regalia and the Stone of Scone, during his triumphal campaign in Scotland in 1296. The regalia and the stone were sent south and deposited in Westminster Abbey but the Black Rood was kept, among other relics, in Edward's chapel. It remained with him until his death in 1307, for an inventory made soon afterwards includes:

Monuments, Rites and Customs belonging or being within the Monastical Church of Durham before the Suppression, written 1593, ed. J. T. Fowler (SS 107; 1902), pp. 6–7.

[4] *The Chronicle of Lanercost 1272–1346,* trans. Herbert Maxwell (Glasgow, 1913), p. 341.

[5] Much of the detail in this paper concerning the Black Rood comes from George Watson, 'The Black Rood of Scotland', *Transactions of the Scottish Ecclesiological Society* 2 (1906–8), pp. 27–46.

[6] *Ibid.,* pp. 37–8.

In a casket sealed above with the seal of the cross: namely, the Cross Neygt ... Likewise the Black Rood of Scotland, constructed of gold, with a gold chain, in a casket with a wooden interior and with its outer side of silver gilded over.[7]

It might be argued that Edward was merely a collector of relics, as were many people at this period. The wardrobe accounts show that Edward did make regular offerings to the relics in his chapel at religious festivals.[8] But it is clear that Edward considered the Black Rood as symbolic of his claims to overlordship in Scotland. When he accepted oaths of loyalty from the nobles of Scotland they swore to him on the Rood. For example, on 26 July 1296 Robert Wisart, bishop of Glasgow, came to Edward at Elgin, renounced the Scottish alliance with France and swore fealty to the English king. He swore on the Cross of Neyth (mentioned in the document quoted above as *Cross Neygt*) and the Black Rood. Later in the year he confirmed his oath before Parliament and again swore on the two crosses to be true to Edward.[9]

The suggestion that Edward conceived of the Black Rood as symbolic of Scotland is reinforced by the inclusion of the Cross of Neyth among the relics in his chapel and its use for oath swearing with the Black Rood. For the cross of Neyth was for the Welsh a symbol akin to that of the Black Rood in Scotland, being appropriated by Edward during the campaign of 1283, when he took effective control of the Principality.

In 1328 Queen Isabella and Roger Mortimer acting for the young Edward III renounced claims to overlordship in Scotland in the Treaty of Northampton. The *Lanercost Chronicle* states that the government intended to return the various objects that Edward I had removed from Scotland as tokens of the peace, and that the Black Rood was in fact returned, but the Londoners were so disgusted by the craven terms of the treaty that they refused to allow the Stone of Scone to leave Westminster.[10] That the Rood was returned at this time is apparently confirmed by its absence from an inventory of the English royal treasuries conducted in 1330.[11]

Before the Battle of Neville's Cross it would appear that the Scots had recovered the Black Rood. Further, that this relic was generally regarded, at the highest levels, as being symbolic of Scotland and Scottish separateness. It is clear that Edward I carried it about with him on his journeys and on campaign, and it seems reasonable to suppose that David II could have

---

[7]   *Ibid.*, p. 40.
[8]   *Ibid.*, p. 40.
[9]   *Ibid.*, pp. 39–40.
[10]   *Chronicle of Lanercost*, trans. Maxwell, p. 260.
[11]   E. L. G. Stones, 'An Addition to the "Rotuli Scotiae"', *Scottish Historical Review* 29 (1950), p. 33.

done the same, especially perhaps on such an important campaign as that of 1346, which it has been stressed was far more than just a raid on England. Thus with the routing of the Scots at Neville's Cross it is possible that the Black Rood was retaken by the English. But *was* this in fact the case? Was the Black Rood really captured at the Battle of Neville's Cross? How reliable is the Durham tradition that the Rood was deposited at the shrine in 1346?

The evidence to answer any of these questions is not complete, and what there is is to some extent contradictory. First, it is not certain that the Black Rood was returned to Scotland in 1328. Although the *Lanercost Chronicle* states categorically that the Black Rood was restored to the Scots, the surviving official documents representing the various stages of the negotiations make no mention of it. It appears that Queen Isabella, going to Scotland to be present at her daughter Joan's marriage to David, was entrusted by the Council with future negotiations with the Scots for the return of estates forfeited from English owners; and that to assist these negotiations she tried to have the Stone of Scone taken north to Berwick, but was thwarted by the refusal of the Londoners to allow its removal.[12] At no point is the Black Rood of Scotland referred to. It could be argued that the Rood was returned at this time, offered by way of an alternative to the Stone of Scone which the queen intended but was unable to offer, and that the official documents are incomplete, as they demonstrably are. However, reference to a further document seems to rule out this possibility. A memorandum published by Palgrave in his *Antient Kalendars . . . of the Exchequer* shows that on 7 January 1346 the Black Rood was taken from the Tower of London and given to the keeper of the king's wardrobe, to be kept 'by the side of the king'.[13] Thus it seems that the Rood was not returned to Scotland in 1328 and could not have been recaptured from the Scots at the Battle of Neville's Cross. In further confirmation of this there is no contemporary commentary on the battle which states that the Black Rood was recaptured. Prior Fossor, the prior of Durham, writing an account of the battle to Bishop Hatfield, who was with Edward III at the siege of Calais, makes no mention of the Black Rood. The chronicler Knighton makes no mention of it either, although the editor of his chronicle feels that he had access to a local Durham source in compiling his commentary, and therefore might have been expected to know.[14] The

---

[12]   Stones, 'An Addition', pp. 32–3 and 34–5.

[13]   The original manuscript transcribed by Palgrave has disappeared, but Professor Stones who rediscovered the printed reference sees no reason to doubt its accuracy; see E. L. G. Stones, 'Allusion to the Black Rood of Scotland in 1346', *Scottish Historical Review* 38 (1959), pp. 174–5.

[14]   *Knighton's Chronicle*, ed. Martin, p. xxxiii.

Lanercost Chronicle, which, as we have seen, bemoans the return of the Rood to Scotland in 1328 also does not comment on its recapture.[15]

That the *Rites* is unreliable in its reporting of events surrounding the Black Rood is confirmed when its further information concerning this relic is considered. The text has a lengthy description of the object it calls the Black Rood, as follows:

> At ye East end of the South Alley (of the choir) adjoyning to the pillar next St Cuthberts Feretorie, next the Quire door on the south side there was a most fair Roode or picture of our Saviour, called the black rood of Scotland with the picture of Mary and Iohn . . . (that was) wonne at the battle of Durham [i.e. Neville's Cross] with the picture of our Lady on the one side of our Saviour and the picture of St Iohn on the other side, the which Rood and pictures were all three very richly wrought in silver, the which were all smoked black over, being large pictures of a Yard and five quarters long, and on every one of their heads, a Crowne of pure bett gold of goldsmiths work...[16]

What is being described here is a large crucifix, 'a yard and five quarters long' with attendant figures of the Virgin and St John. The description goes on to say how the figures are attached to a wainscott panel which is itself decorated. What is being described here is a rood, that is a large three dimensional representation of the Crucifixion of Christ with attendant figures of the Virgin and St John, such as would have been found in every church, most typically above the main or rood screen separating the chancel and nave. There is no indication that this piece is any sort of reliquary. The Black Rood that Edward I took from the Scots was nothing like this. It seems rather to have been a small cross. St Margaret is said to have taken it in her hands at the time of her death. It is further described as being 'about a palm's length', that is about eight inches long. The inventory made at Edward I's death in 1307 confirms this when it says that the Rood was contained in a casket and had a gold chain. The impression gained is that the Black Rood was a smallish object, which could have been worn around the neck. It is possible that the author of the *Rites* is correct and Lord Neville did make a thank-offering to the shrine of St Cuthbert in 1346 and that the gift he gave was a large rood, but the author is mistaken in asserting that this was the Black Rood of Scotland.

It would be possible to discount the claim of the author of the *Rites* that the monastery of Durham held the Black Rood in the later middle ages

---

15   Document c.

16   *Rites of Durham*, ed. Fowler, p. 19. The editor of the *Rites* attempts to harmonise the discrepancies in the accounts of the Black Rood by suggesting that two crosses were captured (p. 210). Watson, 'The Black Rood of Scotland', establishes the true nature of the relic.

but for one additional piece of evidence. There is a list of the relics of the church of Durham, made in 1383, by the monk in charge of the Feretory, Richard de Segbrok. This list itemises the relics kept in the cupboards which at that time were all around St Cuthbert's shrine. In the first cupboard to the south, the list records:

> *In primis*, upon the first or highest shelf...an image of the blessed Virgin Mary, of silver gilt...Item, a black cross, called the Black Rode of Scotland. Item, a cross of crystal, in the custody of the sacrist.[17]

Here, in an official Durham Priory document, is an object called the Black Rood, attached to the shrine of St Cuthbert and kept in a cupboard. The fact that it was kept in a cupboard with other objects suggests that it was a smallish object and not to be confused with the great crucifix described in the *Rites*. There is no description of the casket or any indication that the cross in question was a reliquary. Further, the cross in question is described as black, whilst the 1307 inventory and the 1346 document both refer to a gold cross which is called the Black Rood of Scotland. Despite these discrepancies, here less than forty years after the record of the Rood in the king's treasury in London is a reference to a relic which late sources say was given to the shrine of St Cuthbert in 1346. No further information is forthcoming from contemporary Durham Priory records. On the other hand there is no independent tradition claiming that the Black Rood was held and venerated elsewhere. In 1537, Bellenden published his translation and adaptation of Boece's *History of Scotland* in which he told how the Black Rood, captured by the English at the 'Battle of Durham' (i.e. Neville's Cross), was still preserved at Durham, where it was regarded with the greatest veneration. This repeats the Durham tradition but would suggest that Bellenden had not heard of another. Therefore, however unsatisfactory the state of the evidence, and although the Black Rood cannot have been captured at Neville's Cross, nor deposited at the Shrine as a thank-offering as a result of the battle, there does appear to be a distinct possibility that the Black Rood of Scotland was in Durham in the later middle ages and that it came there sometime between January 1346 when it is last referred to in the king's possession and 1383 when it was included in a Durham relic list.[18]

If it is allowed that the Black Rood was in Durham in the later middle ages but that it was not captured at the Battle of Neville's Cross, some suggestions as to how it reached Durham must be offered. The war with

---

[17] *Extracts from the Account Rolls of the Abbey of Durham*, ed. J. T. Fowler (SS 99–100; 1898–9), II, 426.

[18] It will be obvious that I am entirely dependant on published material for the content of this paper; further discoveries may change the picture as to the history of the Black Rood.

Scotland, beginning with Edward I's campaign in 1296, began a prolonged period when the north-east of England was on a war footing, either providing military support for the king's armies or suffering from border raiding. The monks of Durham were not immune from the effects of this situation; 1346 was not the first time the war had been on their doorstep. For example, in 1314–15 the Scots ravaged Bearpark and destroyed the crops so that the prior was forced to send messengers to other parts of the country to obtain food. In 1322, the Scots were present in such numbers in Yorkshire that the prior was unable to travel south to present his accounts at the Exchequer. The prior was also involved, as one of the king's justiciars, in enforcing in Northumberland observance of the 1331 treaty with the Scots. In the spring of 1333, when war was renewed, he was concerned with organising part of the transport for supplies for the army, whilst in August 1343 he was ordered to collect troops and proceed to the March to repel an expected invasion.[19] The monks too were deeply involved with practical matters concerned with the war and were also affected by the inroads of the Scots. Moreover, their collective aid as a religious body was sought for the successful prosecution of the conflict. In 1320, they were ordered to hold processions and to pray for English success; and from the earliest campaigns the Banner of St Cuthbert, which was popularly held to ward off defeat, was summoned to lead the English army. For example, in 1299–1300 Edward I paid £2 13s. 4d. to 'Dompno William de Gretham, monk of Durham, following the king with the banner of St Cuthbert, in the Scotch war this present year, by gift of the king, to buy him a habit'.[20]

It is clear that the kings recognised that their success was attributable to St Cuthbert's aid. After the triumphant campaign of 1296, whilst he was at Berwick on 16 September, Edward I granted to the church of Durham £40, to secure various religious observances. First, on the two principal feast days of St Cuthbert, namely 20 March and 4 September, 3000 poor were to receive a penny each. Secondly, a priest was to say the mass of the saint every day in the Galilee Chapel, while two great candles each of 20 *lbs* were to burn before his feretory during mass. Thirdly, two smaller lights were to burn before the Banner of St Cuthbert on Sundays and other principal feasts during the celebration of matins and mass at the high altar.[21] Before the Battle of Halidon in 1338, Edward III had vowed that if God gave him the victory he would build a house for thirteen Benedictine monks. After the Scots were defeated he granted to the Bishop of Durham

---

[19]   *VCH Durham*, II, 96–8.
[20]   W. Longstaffe 'The Banner and Cross of St Cuthbert', *Archaeologia Aeliana*, new series, 2 (1858) p. 58.
[21]   *Ibid.*, pp. 57–8.

the advowson of Simonburn church to endow a cell of Durham in Oxford, which was to become Durham College.[22] It is clear that Edward III felt strongly his claims to overlordship in Scotland, as the expression of his views to the Parliament at York in 1332–3 makes clear.[23] That he continued to hold these views seems to be supported by the tenor of the early negotiations for David's release. It is therefore reasonable to suppose that he viewed the Black Rood much as his grandfather had done.

Against this background two possible ways for the Black Rood to reach Durham suggest themselves. First, Edward III may have granted the Black Rood of Scotland to the shrine of St Cuthbert after the Battle of Neville's Cross as a thank-offering, in recognition of the vital contribution that that victory had contributed to his French schemes. Thus the *Rites* could be correct in suggesting that the Black Rood was a gift to the shrine after the battle, but mistaken in attributing the gift to Lord Neville. Given the confused nature of the traditions recorded in the *Rites* and the prominence of the Nevilles as benefactors of the monastery, this mistake is comprehensible. The second possibility is that the Rood was sent to the North before the Battle of Neville's Cross. The 1346 document records that on 7 January it was taken from the treasury in the Tower to be kept 'by the side of the king'. This suggests that Edward III intended to take the Black Rood with him on campaign as his grandfather had done, but he did not depart for France until July. Is it not possible that he wished to have the Rood by him so that it could be delivered to Durham to help in the negotiations which were in prospect or to aid in resisting the expected Scottish invasion?[24] One small piece of evidence suggests that this may have been so. The chronicler Knighton, who seems to have had local sources of information for his account of the battle states:

> The English, placing all their hope in God, exalting the cause of righteousness above death, and having full faith in the sign of the Cross, which was carried before them with their other standards, commended themselves entirely to that divine mercy which never fails, and with the greatest daring gave themselves bravely to the fight.[25]

Longstaffe interprets this as a reference to St Cuthbert's Banner,[26] but it might also be a reference to the Black Rood carried in some conspicuous way on the battlefield.

---

22 *VCH Durham*, II, 98.
23 R. Nicholson, *Edward III and the Scots* (Oxford 1965), pp.100–1.
24 R. White, 'The Battle of Neville's Cross', *Archaeologia Aeliana*, new series, 1 (1857), pp. 271–303.
25 *Knighton's Chronicle*, ed. Martin, p. 69.
26 Longstaffe, 'Banner and Cross', p. 53.

However the Black Rood arrived in Durham it did not play any conspicuous part in subsequent events relating to Scotland. St Cuthbert's Banner was summoned to accompany the English forces in various subsequent campaigns. Records survive for: 1355–6, when it was present for the recovery of Berwick and the 'Burnt Candlemas' campaign; for 1385–6 in Richard II's expedition; for 1400–1 in Henry IV's invasion, when repairs were made to the banner, including the making of a cross for the top 'by order of the Lord King and the Prior'; for 1513–14 when the banner accompanied the Earl of Surrey to Flodden; and in 1522 and 1523.[27] On not one of these occasions is there any evidence that the Black Rood also accompanied the army.

The absence of the Black Rood in the sources is frustrating, but one last piece of evidence may help to account for it. It appears that St Cuthbert's Banner did not display the arms of the see (that is, azure, a cross flory, or, between four lions rampant, argent), but rather St Cuthbert's badge, which was a cross. The history of this badge is obscure but it appears to be ancient, being found before 1346. The *Rites* says that the banner had a red cross but evidence from the depositions made by Robert Aske after the Pilgrimage of Grace in 1536 suggest otherwise. St Cuthbert's banner was carried in that revolt, being in the vanguard at Doncaster. According to Aske, one of the leaders, Lord Darcy, distributed badges of a cross with the five wounds of Christ, but Aske stated that 'as he remembereth that bage with a Blake Crose came first with them of Seint Cutbert Baner.'[28] Is it possible that once in Durham the Black Rood became rapidly equated with the badge of St Cuthbert and so disappeared as a distinct item? This would help to account for the serious confusions in the Durham traditions as exemplified by the *Rites*. The easiest way for this to have occurred is for the Rood to have been attached to St Cuthbert's Banner. It was the right sort of size to have been attached to the top of its staff. We know that on at least two occasions a cross head was made or remade.[29] How easy it would be in those circumstances for a gold cross, called the Black Rood to be lost sight of, leaving only its blackness behind it to colour St Cuthbert's Badge.

---

[27]   *Ibid.*, pp. 60–3.
[28]   *Ibid.*, *passim* but especially p. 63.
[29]   *Ibid.*, pp. 60–1. For the description of the banner in the *Rites*, see p. 26.

The Durham Landscape and the Battle of Neville's Cross

R. A. LOMAS

Armies fight on land, and therefore knowledge of the form and condition of the land at the time of a battle must assist our understanding of what took place. What follows, therefore, is an attempt to establish the nature of the landscape on which the Battle of Neville's Cross was fought, and through which the two opposing armies moved to meet on 17 October 1346. The exercise may as a consequence help to pinpoint where the fighting took place, or at least where it started. The results of the investigation are presented on two maps, one based upon two 2½ inch Second Series Ordnance Survey maps: NZ 24/34 (Durham) and NZ 23/33 (Spennymoor), which cover the land between Durham and Bishop Auckland (ill. 3), the other upon two 6 inch Ordnance Survey maps and depicting in greater detail the ground over which the two armies clashed (ill. 4). They are the product of the application to these maps of data found in medieval sources, particularly the title deeds and estate management records relating to properties owned by the Bishop of Durham and the Cathedral Priory of Durham who were the landlords, immediately or at one remove, of almost all the land involved. Equally important are the plans drawn for the enclosure of Crossgate Moor (1769), Elvet Moor (1771) and Framwellgate Moor and Witton Gilbert (1801).[1]

Although these sources provide a great deal of information, it is not sufficient for a complete and fully accurate picture to be drawn. Nevertheless, what emerges is enough to establish the main outlines and the essential character of the mid-fourteenth-century landscape around Durham. Immediately, two features stand out. One is that the landscape was complex and varied in that it contained not only villages but also hamlets, discrete farms, parks and smaller closes of various shapes and sizes. The other is that all these elements existed in a sea of moorland, so that the overall impression is of a landscape at an intermediate stage of development. In fact, this was so: although some piecemeal enclosure took place after 1346, there were still almost 3000 acres of natural moorland for the three enclosure acts mentioned above to deal with. Not until the early

---

[1] DCDCM.

nineteenth century was the land around Durham finally reduced to individual occupancy and control.

Establishing when the process of enclosure was completed thus presents little difficulty. Determining when it started is a much greater problem. But there are clues. Archaeological investigation in the Browney valley in the immediate neighbourhood of the land on which the events of 17 October 1346 took place points to considerable forest clearance and subsequent cereal cultivation beginning towards the end of the late Iron Age, continuing through the Romano-British period and afterwards until *c.* A.D. 600. Then, however, it appears to have ended rather suddenly, and the land reverted to a natural grass and tree covered condition.[2] Thus, when William of St Calais arrived in Durham as bishop in 1081 and began the Norman revolution in the region, it is likely that much of the land north, west and south of the town was largely, if not entirely, devoid of settlement and in an unenclosed and uncultivated condition. Unfortunately, the omission of Durham from the Domesday Survey of 1086, which, ironically, St Calais may have masterminded,[3] makes it all but impossible to be certain. What tends to support the notion, however, are the numerous references to extensive tracts of moorland in the documents recording grants made by the twelfth- and thirteenth-century bishops to various individuals and institutions.

The earliest of these grants known to us was made in August 1128 when Bishop Ranulf Flambard, recognising the imminence of death, restored to the monks of his cathedral several disputed properties he had seized from them earlier in his pontificate. All were identified by name, except that described as 'the land beyond the bridge at Durham'.[4] By this he meant Framwellgate Bridge (Durham's other bridge, Elvet Bridge, was not built until much later in the century) which he had caused to be constructed over ten years previously. The priory's reaction was to reinforce its possession by creating the Borough of Crossgate, which was sufficiently developed by 1144 to be mentioned among the properties badly damaged in the fighting between the forces of the two rivals for the bishopric, William Cumin, the King of Scotland's Chancellor, and the priory's choice, William of Ste Barbe, dean of York.[5] The existence of the borough by this date is also supported by the Norman architecture of its church, which was

2   A. M. Donaldson and J. Turner 'A Pollen Diagram from Hallowell Moss near Durham City', *Journal of Biogeography* 4 (1977), pp. 25–33.
3   P. Chaplais, 'William of St. Calais and the Domesday Book Survey', in *Domesday Studies*, ed J. C. Holt (London, 1987), pp. 65–77.
4   *Durham Episcopal Charters 1071–1152*, ed. H.S.Offler (SS 179; 1968), p. 107.
5   R. B. Dobson, *Durham Priory 1400–1450* (Cambridge, 1973), p. 40.

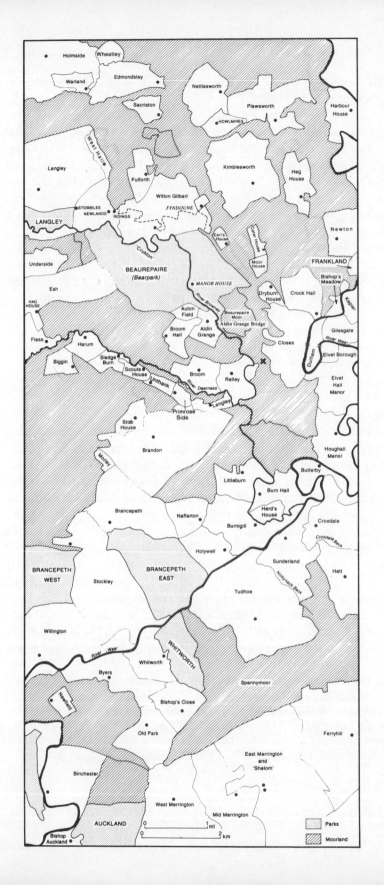

Holmside Wheatley
Warland Edmondsley
Sacriston
Nettlesworth
HOWLMIRES
Plawsworth
Harbour House
Langley
Fulforth
Kimblesworth
Hag House
Witton Gilbert
STOBBILEE NEWLANDS RIDINGS *FYNDOUNE*
LANGLEY
Earl's House
Carter House
Moor House
Newton
FRANKLAND
Underside
'Crukton'
BEAUREPAIRE
(Bearpark)
MANOR HOUSE
River Browney
Bishop's Meadow
Dryburn House
Crook Hall
Esh
HAG HOUSE
Auton Field
Broom Hall
Aldin Grange
Beaurepaire Moor
Aldin Grange Bridge
Closes
Gilesgate
River Wear
Durham
Elvet Borough
Flass
Harum
Siedge Burn
Scouts House
Unthank
Broom
Relley
Elvet Hall Manor
Biggin
River Deerness
Langley
Primrose Side
Houghall Manor
Stob House
Brandon
Morley
Littleburn
Butterby
Brancepeth
Nafferton
Burn Hall
Herd's House
Croxdale
Burnigill
Croxdale Beck
BRANCEPETH WEST
BRANCEPETH EAST
Stockley
Holywell
Sunderland
Nickynack Beck
Hett
Tudhoe
Willington
River Wear
Byers
Whitworth
WHITWORTH
Spennymoor
Newfield
Bishop's Close
Old Park
Ferryhill
Binchester
East Merrington and 'Shelom'
West Merrington
Mid Merrington
AUCKLAND
Bishop Auckland

0 .... 1 ml
0 .... 2 km

Parks
Moorland

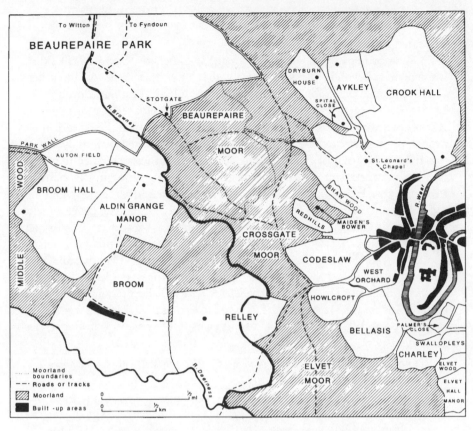

Inside the map:

To Witton · To Fyndoun

BEAUREPAIRE PARK

DRYBURN HOUSE · AYKLEY · CROOK HALL

R. Browney

STOTGATE · BEAUREPAIRE

SPITAL CLOSE

PARK WALL

AUTON FIELD

MOOR

St. Leonard's Chapel

WOOD

BROOM HALL

ALDIN GRANGE MANOR

SHAW WOOD

REDHILLS · MAIDEN'S BOWER

R. Wear

CROSSGATE

MOOR · CODESLAW

MIDDLE

WEST ORCHARD

BROOM

HOWLCROFT

RELLEY

BELLASIS · PALMER'S CLOSE

SWALLOPLEYS

CHARLEY

ELVET WOOD

R. Deerness

ELVET MOOR

ELVET HALL MANOR

Moorland boundaries
Roads or tracks
Moorland
Built-up areas

0 ... ½ ml
0 ... ½ km

Illustration 4 (above): Map of the area of Durham City, Neville's Cross and Bearpark, *c.*1346.

Illustration 3 (opposite): Map of the countryside west of Durham City, *c.*1346.

dedicated to St Margaret of Antioch.[6]

The northern boundary of Flambard's concession was the Mill Burn. Immediately beyond this stream was the land that came to be called Framwellgate, where the bishops sited the suburb of their Borough of Durham, the eastward expansion of which was blocked by another of Bishop Flambard's foundations, the Borough of Gilesgate. Flambard in all probability was also responsible for the aptly named settlement of Newton, two miles north-east of Framwellgate Bridge, the earliest reference to which occurs in a document issued by him in June 1112.[7] All in all, it is hard to resist the conclusion that Flambard's decision to build the bridge where he did was a necessary first move in a policy of opening up for development the empty ground to the west and north of Durham. Newton and Crossgate apart, the only other settlements that may have existed in this area before 1150, to judge by their names, were Witton, Plawsworth and Kimblesworth. This, however, is speculation. Firm evidence of their existence does not emerge until the 1180s when Bishop Hugh of le Puiset commissioned the survey of the episcopal estates that became known as Boldon Book.[8] This document also reveals the existence of five other settlements:

Holmside, where the tenant's services were connected with the bishop's hunting activities.

Fulforth, which was linked with Witton. Both places were shortly to be granted to Gilbert de la Ley, whose name still distinguishes Witton near Durham from Witton le Wear.

'Croketon', which lay on the south side of the River Browney opposite Witton and which also came into the possession of Gilbert de la Ley but was destroyed a few years later.

Langley, with its clearance name, was probably of recent origin, an impression reinforced by the fact that it was not referred to as village before 1232.[9]

Edmondsley, which also has a clearance name. Recent origin here is suggested by its very small rent, 32d.

Other evidence reveals the existence of three further settlements at this time: Aldingrange (then *Aldingrig*), Broom and Relley occupying a

[6]   N. Pevsner (revised E. Williamson), *The Buildings of England: County Durham* (Harmondsworth, 1985), pp. 220–1.

[7]   *Durham Episcopal Charters*, ed. Offler, pp. 64–5.

[8]   *Boldon Book*, ed. and trans. D. Austin (Chichester, 1982), pp. 46–9. The editor incorrectly identifies 'Croketon' as Crookhall and so repeats the error in Surtees, II, 353–4.

[9]   P. Clack, 'The Browney Valley', *Transactions of the Architectural and Archaeological Society of Durham and Northumberland*, new series, 6 (1982), p. 13.

continuous piece of ground between the rivers Browney and Deerness. This evidence relates to the attempt by Bishop Hugh's son, Henry, to establish a cell of the Augustinian canonry of Guisborough at Baxterwood (then *Bakestaneford*) on the western bank of the Browney on what was described by the bishop as 120 acres of waste next to the cultivated land of Aldingrange.[10] This latter, which eventually became a manorial farm, was described as a village to which the tenant farmers of Broom and Relley owed service.[11] The fact that all three were small in area (under 200 acres), together with their clearance names, argues, although it does not prove, recent origin.

The prospect of a rival on the doorstep immediately induced a sense of outrage and fear in the minds of the Durham monks, and their resistance to the proposed development was successful to the point that, not only was the Baxterwood project abandoned, but the younger Puiset made over to the Cathedral Priory the property he had accumulated which was then used to endow the cell the priory was founding on the site of St Godric's hermitage at Finchale on the eastern edge of Framwellgate Moor opposite Cocken.[12] And it is clear that both the original land on which the cell was built, and the additional land gifted by Bishop Richard Kellaw in 1311, were carved out of the moor.[13]

Before 1200, therefore, a dozen settlements had been established in the moorland north and west of Durham. Almost exactly two hundred years after Bishop Hugh's survey, a successor, Thomas Hatfield, repeated the exercise. His survey reveals that in the meantime ten further substantial settlements had come into existence: Wheatley, Warland, Harbour House, Earl's House, Moor House, Dryburn House, Nettlesworth Manor, Howlmires Manor, Wast Hall (not yet identified) and an unnamed farm of 77 acres. Also, Crook Hall,[14] Stobbilee,[15] Sacriston and Fyndoun[16] and Hag House and Cater House[17] are known to have been created by this date. These settlements had three things in common. They were, or appear to have been, in single, not community, occupancy; they were all on episcopal

---

[10] *The Priory of Finchale*, ed. J. Raine (SS 6; 1837), pp. 8–9.

[11] *Ibid.*, p. 23.

[12] *Ibid.*, pp. 23–4.

[13] *Ibid.*, pp. 21 and 25.

[14] *Bishop Hatfield's Survey*, ed. W. Greenwell (SS 32; 1856), pp. 76 and 83–8.

[15] Surtees, II. 334.

[16] Clack, 'Browney Valley', p. 13.

[17] *Registrum Palatinum Dunelmense: The Register of Richard de Kellawe, Lord Palatine and Bishop of Durham*, ed. T. D. Hardy (RS 62; 4 vols., London, 1873–8), II, 1132–3. This reveals that the original grant was made by Bishop Bek, i.e. before 1311.

land and so must be assumed to be episcopal foundations; and they came into existence between c.1200 and 1315. The earliest was probably Crook Hall, which is known to have existed in 1217,[18] and the latest were Harbour House and Sacriston, both of which arose from the generosity of Bishop Richard Kellaw, who early in his pontificate gifted the requisite moorland to, respectively, his own brother, Patrick, and the sacrist of the Cathedral Priory.[19] In addition to these large settlements, almost all of which bore names, Bishop Hatfield's surveyors recorded under 'Framwellgate' and 'Newton' seventy unnamed enclosures with a combined area of at least 550 acres. Most of them were very small, as is indicated by their average size of just over 7 acres. And a similar development had occurred in the priory's land adjacent to Crossgate Borough, although here, as Illustration 4 shows, there were several large closes with names. Definite dates of origin cannot be assigned to these closes, but sometime in the thirteenth century is almost certain. What was happening around Durham was in fact part of a Europe-wide increase in settlement and cultivation which was basically a function of population growth and expanding economic activity.

If the origin of these holdings, large and small, is largely unrecorded, this was not true for the most spectacular development, which was to be at the very centre of the events of 17 October 1346, the park known as Beaurepaire (today Bearpark). It belonged to the Cathedral Priory, and at over 1500 acres was one of the largest parks in medieval England. The land out of which it was formed was obtained from two sources.[20] The first was Gilbert de la Ley, the lord of Witton, who late in the twelfth century made over to the monks 60 acres of land in Witton, and then the entire village of 'Croketon', which the priory shortly cleared to make way for a cattle farm. To this Bishop Nicholas Farnham (1242–8) and Bishop Robert Stichill (1261–74) added extensive tracts of moorland. Formal permission to empark was issued by the latter in 1267, but some nine years earlier the then prior, Bertram Middleton, had built a manor house as his retirement home. It was in this building, which his father, Robert Bruce, had damaged during his raid in 1315, that King David of Scotland would lodge on the night before the battle.[21] The park was eventually surrounded by a wall, although this was not completed until some years into the fourteenth century.[22]

---

[18] Surtees, IV, 137.

[19] *Registrum Palatinum Dunelmense,* ed. Hardy, II, 1127 and 1148.

[20] The documents relating to the creation of Beaurepaire are comprehensively calendared in an unpublished handlist prepared in 1978 by M.G.Snape.

[21] *Historiae Dunelmensis Scriptores Tres,* ed. J.Raine (SS 9; 1839), p. 96.

[22] This was certainly after 1311 when Bishop Richard Kellaw granted to the monks a ten-foot wide strip of land along the north-east side of the park to

By 1346, therefore, it is clear that considerable inroads had been made into the moorland to the north and west of Durham. About the land to the south less can, and in fact need, be said. This is particularly so with regard to the area in the angle between the River Wear and the River Deerness which was part of the Neville estate based upon Brancepeth. As far as is known, none of this land was involved in the events of 17 October 1346, except Burnigill, which would have been entered by both Scots and English when crossing Sunderland Bridge. Immediately south of the Wear were three settlements, all known to have existed before 1200.[23] The oldest was almost certainly Croxdale, the Scandinavian suffix of its name indicating an origin well before the Conquest. This notion is supported by its being the site of the chapel of ease serving this part of Elvet parish. Sunderland was probably founded later, while Beautrove, the original French name of Butterby, points to a post-Conquest origin. To the west of these settlements the farms of Burn Hall and Burnigill probably came into being in the thirteenth century.

Between Croxdale and Bishop Auckland lay a group of settlements abutting a large tract of waste known as Spennymoor. All of them had grazing rights in this moor, and in the generation before 1315 all of them had been colonising adjacent parts of the moor and subjecting them to cultivation.[24] The oldest of these settlements was Merrington. Documents of the early and mid-twelfth century speak of Merrington in the singular; but another document written in the last decade of that century refers to two Merringtons, probably East Merrington and West Merrington (now Kirk Merrington and Westerton).[25] Mid Merrington (now Middlestone) was created between c. 1200 and 1270.[26] Two of the other settlements, Ferryhill and Hett, like the three Merringtons, belonged to the Cathedral Priory, while Whitworth was a member of the bishop's estate and Tudhoe was part of the Neville estate centred on Brancepeth: all four townships were in existence well before 1200.

Not far beyond Spennymoor to the south-west lay Auckland Park, extending north-eastwards from the bishop's manor house. It was in this park that the English army camped the night before the battle, and from which they set out, possibly across the open ground of Spennymoor,

---

enable them to build a stone wall: *Registrum Palatinum Dunelmense*, ed. Hardy, II 1141–2.

[23] *VCH Durham*, III, 161–2.

[24] *Scriptores Tres*, ed. Raine, pp. 74 and cclxx; *Durham Cathedral Priory Rentals I: Bursar's Rentals*, ed. R. A. Lomas and A. J. Piper (SS 198; 1989), pp. 62–5.

[25] *Durham Episcopal Charters*, ed. Offler, pp. 8, 18, 27, and 57.

[26] *Durham Bursar's Rentals*, ed. Lomas and Piper, p. 24.

towards the river crossing at Sunderland Bridge. It was on this march that they clashed with the Scottish foraging party under Sir William Douglas.

Before looking more closely at the possible battle site, three changes in the course of rivers must be noted. At unknown dates, and possibly after 1346, the Wear near Butterby and the Browney near Witton broke through narrow necks of land to form ox-bow lakes. The change in the course of the Wear near Houghall, however, took place in the mid-fifteenth century, well after the 1346 campaign. It is also important to note the existence of three stone bridges: those over the Wear at Framwellgate and Sunderland; and that over the Browney at Aldingrange under which local legend erroneously had the Scottish king hiding after the battle and betrayed by his shadow across the water.

Illustration 4 (p. 69) is intended to give a more precise and detailed depiction of the ground over which the two armies fought. Of greatest significance is what was called Beaurepaire Moor. The priory's version of its history was that it was the ground extending westwards from Crossgate Borough as far as the park boundary, and that the inhabitants of Crossgate had no inherent grazing rights in it. These, however, were granted to them by the monks as an act of gratuitous generosity in that part of the moor between the closes adjacent to Crossgate and the road running northwards towards the head of the Mill Burn. They were, in fact, given permission to fence off this land along a line next to an ancient ditch close to the road.[27] In effect, the priory was dividing the moor into two parts, Beaurepaire Moor and Crossgate Moor. The demarcation line was almost certainly that of the western boundary of Crossgate Moor on the 1769 enclosure plan, which is still clearly discernible as the hedge running northwards from the bottom of Tollhouse Road, behind the houses at Moor Edge to the head of Club Lane, and thence to the park boundary. This division would appear to have been made before 1312, perhaps at the same time as the priory and Bishop Anthony Bek (1283–1311) agreed the boundary between their respective settlements of Crossgate and Framwellgate.[28]

The importance of this becomes fully apparent when the contents of the news-letter sent by Prior John Fossor to Bishop Hatfield, who was with King Edward III in France, recounting the dramatic events of October 1346, are considered. Fossor stated explicitly that the Scots army, having spent the night of 16 October within the park (and he was at pains to stress

[27] *Feodarium Prioratus Dunelmensis,* ed. W.Greenwell (SS 58; 1872), p. 193.
[28] *Ibid.,* p. 192.

that none of them were outside the park) were drawn up for battle on Beaurepaire Moor.[29] The unavoidable conclusion would therefore seem to be that David II formed his battles on grounds which are now Arbour House farm and Moorsley Banks.[30] This covers not far short of 200 acres and is therefore a large area for a relatively small army; consequently, it is a matter of speculation as to which part of it he selected. Perhaps most likely is the southerly part, where the ground slopes steeply south-eastwards from Stotgate, one of the main entrances to the park, to a sike which runs parallel to the present A167 and into the Browney. The western bank of this sike rises almost vertically to the A167, and so presents a definite barrier to rapid movement. Here the Scots would have occupied rising ground facing the line of the English approach while covering their own line of retreat. A few yards further north the ravine of the sike peters out and the two moors run together without physical interruption.

What were these moors like? Obviously a fully accurate answer is unattainable, but there are some indications. It is unlikely that there were many trees; equally there would have been a great deal of rough grass. And, there is evidence of whins and ling. The presence of the former is attested by the decision of the priory, probably in or around 1425, to enclose 62 acres of Beaurepaire Moor. The field they created was known as the Great Close next to Stotgate, but also, and significantly, by the more colloquial name of Whinney Close.[31] And as if to underline this clue, whins still grow on the steeper uncultivatable banks of the sike between the A167 and Arbour House farm. As regards ling, its presence is proven by the fact that between 1331 and 1337 the monks cut almost 2700 thraves of ling on Beaurepaire Moor, ostensibly for fuel, but also perhaps to clear the moor to improve its grazing potential.[32] Ironically, and of course unintentionally, they may have prepared the battle ground. Finally, it is worth considering that the moorland between Durham and Beaurepaire may have looked much like the present Waldridge Fell, the only stretch of moor between Durham and Chester le Street never to have been enclosed.

---

[29] *Scriptores Tres*, ed. Raine, p. ccccxxxiv.

[30] Moorsley Banks lay between the Tollhouse Road to Aldingrange Bridge Road and the Browney. It was enclosed in 1401 and leased to a John Moreby, hence its original name, Moreby Banks: DCDCM, Bursar's Account Roll 1401/2 (unpublished).

[31] DCDCM, Beaurepaire Manor Accounts (unpublished).

[32] DCDCM, Bursar's Account Rolls 1332/3–1336/7 (unpublished).

It is also possible to identify, although not with absolute certainty, some of the the roads or tracks which traversed these moors and which may have played a part in the events of October 1346. Five related specifically to Beaurepaire, three leading from Durham to its manor house, and two leading away from it towards the north and west.[33]

1. From Durham: along Allergate, up Redhills Lane, down Tollhouse Road, across the land of Arbour House to the park entrance at Stotgate.

2. From Durham: up Castle Chare and Back Western Hill, along Fieldhouse Lane, by the vennel to the A167, along Club Lane on the opposite side of this road to the field track to Stotgate.

3. From Durham: up Castle Chare and Back Western Hill, along Fieldhouse Lane to the A167 at Western Lodge, across the A167 and up the lane to Aden Cottage. Another track ran from Western Lodge to Sniperley Park, whence it followed the park wall towards Witton, Lanchester and the north.

4. From the manor house: a path ran almost due north and left the park at Sleights House farm in the direction of Fyndoun and Sacriston.

5. From the manor house: a path followed the north bank of the Browney to Witton from where roads ran in several directions

Another important track ran from the head of Crossgate, up Crossgate Peth to Neville's Cross where it divided into three branches:

a) northwards by St Johns Road to the A167 and so to join the road coming up Fieldhouse Lane;

b) westwards down Neville's Cross Bank to the Browney at Stone Bridge;

c) southwards across Crossgate Moor and then Elvet Moor to cross the Wear by Sunderland Bridge.

---

[33] The paths marked on the current Ordnance Survey Pathfinder maps largely conform to those on earlier maps, which raises a strong presumption of antiquity. The present roads between the ancient closes must by definition be at least as old as those closes.

This reconstuction of the landscape of 1346 does not, indeed cannot, identify the battlefield; but it does help to narrow the ground on which the events of 17 October were played out.

The Monument at Neville's Cross, Co. Durham

J. LINDA DRURY

Neville's Cross, Nevilles Cross or Neville Cross was *not* a monument first erected by Ralph Neville, lord of Brancepeth and Raby, to mark the victory over an army under King David of Scotland by an English army, in which Neville himself was a prominent leader, at a battle in the vicinity in 1346. There was already an existing cross, which was replaced by a more elaborate one, traditionally by Ralph Neville. The cross stands, as many ancient markers do, on a watershed, this one being just over 300 feet, about 100 metres, above sea level on the ridge between the Wear and Browney valleys just west of Durham City and it has given its name to the surrounding suburb.

Mentions of the battle at Neville's Cross in the poetry of Laurence Minot and other anonymous contemporary poets,[1] as well as chronicle-writers, imply an existing landmark because to locate an important battle by reference to a completely new and still little-known monument would have needed further explanation.

In considering the monument let us now look at the site of the cross and at human activity in the area down the years.[2] The Neville's Cross is a man-made landmark, a way-marker standing today at the junction of roads. On looking back to see how long there has been a junction here, we find two ancient roads. One which is not now visible comes in from Brancepeth and Brandon and the other is the 'great north road' running west of Durham City and becoming, about five miles further north, the main street of Roman Chester-le-Street. The first of these, a Roman road, runs from the south-west from Binchester Roman camp near Bishop Auckland, via Brancepeth, to Neville's Cross. A Roman glass bottle and bowl were found at Relly, Broompark, near Neville's Cross, a few hundred yards from this

---

[1]   *The Poems of Laurence Minot*, ed. Joseph Hall (Oxford, 1887), p. 31 and appendix, pp. 106 and 111.

[2]   The only prehistoric find noted near Neville's Cross is a bronze age uncisted cremation burial within a collared urn, near Stonebridge, a few hundred yards west of the cross. Durham Sites and Monuments Record, no. 555, information from Durham County Archaeologist's Office at Bowes Museum, Barnard Castle, County Durham.

road.[3] This road was excavated along several points by Richard Wright of the Department of Classics at the University of Durham in 1937.[4] If one maps the five points where Wright excavated sections across this road between old Brancepeth and Brandon station (sites between 4 and 2 miles from the Neville's Cross) and joins up the points and produces the line eastwards towards Durham City, the line runs up to the Neville's Cross, although the road itself must have deviated a bit at the foot of the ridge on which the cross stands in order to use a good crossing over the River Browney, a tributary of the Wear. This road probably entered the future site of Durham City down what is now Crossgate Peth, then down Crossgate and so to the Wear and the ford later called Horse Hole. Ivan Margary in 1967 conjectured that the Roman road from the south-east, Sedgefield and Coxhoe (A177) approached the future site of Durham City near Old Durham, where a Roman bath house and other remains have been excavated, crossed the site of Durham City at fords approximately where the New Elvet Bridge and Leazes Bridge (by the Horse Hole ford) now stand, then followed an older route northwards up Milburngate to Framwellgate Moor where it deviated to the right to proceed on a clear line north through Pity Me and Chester-le-Street to Wreckenton and the Tyne crossing.[5]

Since then, no more archaeological work on Margary's conjecture or on other alignments of Roman roads in the Durham City area has been done. However, if Margary's alignment had been the only Roman crossing of the site of Durham City, it would have made an awkward route for any through traffic from Roman Chester-le-Street towards Roman Binchester, because it would have necessitated the descent from Framwellgate to the Wear and the ascent from the Wear up Crossgate to regain the ridge between the Browney and the Wear. No Roman amenity has been identified in the old urban area of Durham City which might have attracted travellers in Roman times down to the site for its own sake. However, if a line is drawn south from Chester-le-Street's long Front Street, formerly the

3   For Roman Chester-le-Street, see P. A. G. Clack, *Chester-le-Street: A Report on the History and Archaeology of the Town* (Archaeological Unit for North-East England; Newcastle upon Tyne, 1980). For the Roman glass bottle, see Durham Sites and Monuments Record, no. 1302. 1 am grateful to Norman Emery and Samantha Middleton for this information.

4   For the Roman road from Binchester direction, see R. P. Wright, 'The Roman Branch Road from Binchester to the North-East', *Archaeologia Aeliana*, 4th series, 15 (1938), pp. 362–8, and I. D. Margary *Roman Roads in Britain* (2nd edn, London, 1967), route 83.

5   Margary, *Roman Roads*, route 80. For Old Durham three reports, 1944, 1951 and 1953, on excavations there, by I.A. Richmond, T. Romans, R.P. Wright and J.P. Gillam, appear in *Archaeologia Aeliana* series 4 vols. 22, 29 & 31.

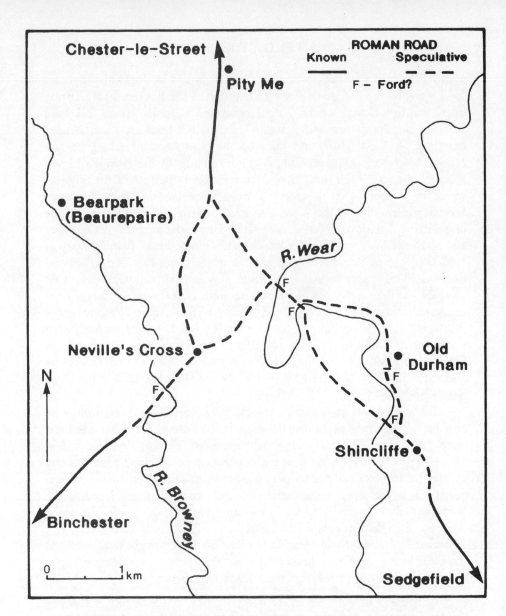

Illustration 5: Roman roads in the area of Durham City, known and inferred, after Wright and Margary, *Roman Roads*, fig. 3 (see p. 79, note 4).

Roman road, south through Pity Me and continued south past Margary's deviation point, it runs west of Durham City, keeping height and a desirable commanding view on Framwellgate and Crossgate Moors and runs to Neville's Cross on the ridge between the rivers, an ideal route for those travelling south in the Binchester rather than the Sedgefield direction. It seems likely that there was a stretch of Roman road, running from Framwellgate Moor to meet the Roman road coming in towards Neville's

Cross from the west from Binchester, which did not deviate down into the Durham City site (a route 'avoiding the city centre') and that this route survived, or was reinstated, along the road past Neville's Cross in use today. Where these two ancient routes from the north and from the south-west would have crossed or joined, there stands the Neville's Cross. Perhaps therefore the first monument at Neville's Cross was a Roman milestone.

What other ancient routes may have passed this way? In a paper of 1987 about the community or congregation of St Cuthbert under their bishop, at Chester-le-Street from 883 to 995, Eric Cambridge considered the route between Lindisfarne and York, the possible stages of that route and the distribution of sculptured stones found mostly near the Roman roads forming it.[6] As the community's route, which predated their move to Durham in 995, probably followed the Roman road from Chester-le-Street southwards, it could be that churchmen, regular travellers along a route skirting the later site of Durham City on the west, replaced a pagan Roman marker at Neville's Cross with a Christian sculptured high cross. Even if such a pagan Roman marker in a prominent place lay a little off their regular route, they might have seen fit to give it a Christian aspect, as was done with other pagan sites and festivals. A generation or two before 1891 'sculptured' stones had been noticed built into the walls of the cow byre of Neville's Cross toll house as is mentioned in connection with a drawing of 1891 described later in this paper. Some may have been pre-Conquest.

In what other ways, as well as a road marker, was the cross a landmark? In the middle ages the site of the Neville's Cross lay a few yards from the north-western boundary of a roughly circular piece of land belonging to Durham Priory's estates, named Howlcroft or Holcroft. Circular boundaries tend to be ancient ones. When the Benedictine Priory's forerunners, the community of St Cuthbert, settled with his body in Durham in 995, there was at that time no division between the lands owned by the bishop and those owned by the rest who became eventually the Benedictine prior and convent. The community of St Cuthbert then owned most of the land immediately west of Durham City. An existing cross could have been used as a reference point when William of St Calais, bishop of Durham (1081–96), put in motion the division of the estates when the interests of the Norman bishops and the local monks, under the prior, divided. This large round plot of some 25 acres, the Howlcroft, stands out among the more angular surrounding boundaries of the smaller

---

6   Eric Cambridge, 'Why did the Community of St. Cuthbert settle at Chester-le-Street?' in *St Cuthbert, his Cult and his Community*, ed. G. Bonner, D. Rollason and C. Stancliffe (Woodbridge, 1989), pp. 367–86. For sculptured stones in cow byre, see p. 90.

fields which abut upon it, boundaries which appear to accommodate the pre-existing Howlcroft. The land to the west and south of Howlcroft was open moorland until the Crossgate Moor Inclosure Award of 1770.[7] The land to the north and east had been enclosed piecemeal long before. The Howlcroft being an ancient enclosure belonging to Durham Priory, a marker on its boundary is likely also to be ancient. However, research has yet to establish how early Howlcroft was enclosed and whether its boundary ever had the cross lying exactly upon it. During the later middle ages Howlcroft was a hay meadow, kept hedged and ditched and duly mown, the hay being brought to the priory.[8] It belonged to the estate of the almoner of the priory but was leased by him to the bursar, the rent in 1536–7 being 60s. p.a..

Now the cross will be considered in relation to the roadway. The old Howlcroft boundary (roughly Archery Rise today) comes to the road on the *south* side of the road opposite the Neville's Cross, whereas the cross itself now stands on the *north* side. The cross was described in a 1560 charter as standing on the south side of the road.[9] However, later travellers passed by on both the north and south sides of it and the Crossgate Moor inclosure plan of 1770 shows the cross out in the road, more towards the north than the south side. In 1838 the Crossgate tithe plan showed it similarly out in the road.[10] However, it should be borne in mind that on open unenclosed moorland, before roads were confined between kerbs and under tarred surfaces, the exact path of a road would deviate from side to side to avoid ruts, mud etc., so that it is likely to have been the roadway that moved, not the cross. It stood on the road and in the road and travellers flowed round its steps which were designed to be walked up on all four sides. Its exact position in relation to the roadway was not important till other boundaries right beside it became fixed and the area of roadway resulting from the enclosure and turnpike movements was found to be too narrow. In 1903 the cross was moved (north-westwards) a few yards, but so little that no

[7]   For the Howlcroft boundary, see above, ill. 4; and Ordnance Survey 25" Durham sheet 27/1 (1st edn), and Crossgate Moor Inclosure Award 1770 among the documents of the Durham Cathedral, Dean and Chapter Muniments (DCDCM), deposited with Durham University Library, Archives and Special Collections (ASC), 5 The College, Durham City.

[8]   For Howlcroft meadow see, numerous references in *Extracts from the Account Rolls of the Abbey of Durham*, ed. J. T. Fowler (3 vols., SS 99, 100 and 103; 1898–1900). Howlcroft was part of the Corps Land of the Third Prebendary of Durham Cathedral. See ASC, Durham University Surveyors Deposit bundle 107.

[9]   For the 1560 charter, see DCDCM, Loc. 37.73.

[10]   For the Crossgate Tithe Plan ASC, Durham Diocesan Records (hereafter DDR).

difference appears between the 25" Ordnance survey plans, editions of 1896 and 1915, before and after this removal.[11] That it was moved at all shows how far it had sunk by then in public consciousness, when one considers the penalties meted out in earlier centuries to those who tampered with boundary markers or mere stones. Between 1915 and 1939 the road at the Neville's Cross was widened again but examination of the Ordnance Survey 25" plans shows that open land was taken at the south side on this occasion.

Neville's Cross, Framwellgate Cross, a lead cross at the junction of Claypath and Tinklers Lane, Philipson's Cross, Charley Cross and perhaps other crosses standing in the medieval period on roads approaching Durham City from the west, north, east and south sides,[12] may have marked significant steps in the approach to the sanctuary in Durham Cathedral, though the marker or cross at the junction at Neville's Cross possibly predates the cathedral founded 995 and its sanctuary in Durham. Tradition has it that pilgrims from the west and others entering and leaving Durham would touch the Neville's Cross. Pilgrims at the shrine of St James at Compostella in Spain still touch a certain stone on arrival. Perhaps touching over centuries contributed to the present worn state of the carved socket of the cross.

The Neville's Cross stands at the top of a bank down which one travels eastwards into Durham City through the Borough of Crossgate, part of the priory's 'Old Borough' which in c.1120 was linked to Bishop Flambard's own borough on the peninsula by his Framwellgate Bridge. The top part of this bank is called Crossgate Peth and the lower part, with the bridge at the foot, is Crossgate. Margaret Camsell noted that in Canterbury it seemed to be usual to refer to a street by its destination rather than by a name and that looks likely in the case of Crossgate, the road leading to the

---

[11] For the moving of Neville's Cross, see *VCH Durham*, III, 146, and Ordnance Survey Durham 27/1 (editions of 1896, 1915 and 1939).

[12] Charley Cross, Phillipson's Cross and one in the market place appear in *The County Palatine of Durham*, surveyed by Captain Armstrong and engraved by Thomas Jefferys (1768 and 1791). See ASC, Halmote Court Records (HC), Msc. Map no. 155. For the lead cross see Margaret M. Camsell, 'The Development of a Northern Town in the Later Middle Ages: The City of Durham. c.1250–1540' (unpubl. D. Phil. thesis, University of York, 1985). The supplement to the thesis is an unpaginated volume of maps. The lead cross is marked on the 'Conjectural Boundaries of Tenements in Clayport, Borough of Durham'. The sites of Neville's and Framwellgate crosses are shown on 25" OS sheet Durham 27/1 (1st edn) and Charley and Phillipsons on 27/5 by the New Inn and by the later Mountjoy roundabout at the south end of Hallgarth Street.

cross, Neville's Cross.[13] The wording of the lease of 1560 of a tenement, 'on the southe syde of the said croisgait next to Nevell Cross', also suggests that the street was named Crossgate after a cross at Neville's Cross. The first firmly dated occurrence of the name of *Crossgathe* borough is between 1272 and 1285 and of *Crossegate* the street is in 1291.[14]

The first firm documentary evidence of the Neville's Cross monument comes in 1323, before the battle was fought. Among the muniments of Durham Priory property are two deeds from that year regarding the same croft of land in Durham, described as lying between two roads – on one side, one which ran behind the West Orchard and on the other one which *ducit versus le Nevillecrosse ex parte altera* ('leads to the Neville Cross on the other side').[15] In centuries past before Land Registries were established, owners preserved all the deeds of their property, as these survivals from 1323 show, not just the last two or three transactions. To help in the clear identification of a property in deeds for future generations, well-known landmarks of long standing and supposed permanence were used as reference points and in 1323 Neville's Cross was already in that category.[16] Similarly the victorious battle was named after a monument about which many generations of travellers and soldiers to the borders of Scotland would know. The naming of the battle after the cross also argues for the importance at that time of the route on which it stood. So, before the battle in 1346 there was already at Neville's Cross, a marker known possibly to Roman soldiers, Anglo-Saxon priests, soldiers and later travellers, and certainly to the Benedictine monks and townsfolk of Durham.

One boundary on which the Neville's Cross does not stand is that of Neville property. However, it does stand on the road between Durham

---

[13] Camsell, 'Development of a Northern Town', I, 57, who failed to make this connection in the case of Crossgate, which she thought was so called because it had a crossroads at each end – but that description applies to many streets (*op. cit.*, II(a), 44–5). She accepted that there was a road on the alignment of Crossgate before the advent of the Borough of Crossgate, which was part of the Old Borough, the settlements of which she described as being linear because they 'spread along the main routes into Durham: South Street, Crossgate and Aluertongate, Milburnegate' (*op. cit.*, I, 43). Early deeds relating to Crossgate are listed and discussed *ibid.*, II, 44–117 (Old Borough – Crossgate).

[14] For *Crossgathe*, c. 1272–85, see ASC, DCDCM, Msc.Ch.2447. For *Crossegate*, 1291, see ASC, DCDCM, Msc. Ch. 1966.

[15] ASC, DCDCM, Msc.Ch. 1976 and 1977.

[16] There is a comparable example from c.1200, when Bishop Philip of Poitiers granted to Henry of Wales land at Softley, County Durham, using a standing stone to define the boundary (ASC, DCDCM, Msc. Ch. 6861).

Castle and Priory and the Nevilles' Brancepeth Castle some four miles away, a road along which this prominent, colourful local family often came to Durham on business or pleasure, sometimes with over-large retinues and over-loud horns, to pay their dues for Raby, including venison, to the Prior and to claim extravagant entertainment from him.[17] The Nevilles held land also of the Bishop of Durham.[18] The family was proud, ambitious and active in affairs. The leader of the house in 1346 was Ralph Neville, fourth baron of Raby and Brancepeth, one of the most efficient and forceful of his family.

In the name the Neville Cross, Nevilles or Neville's Cross, the terminal s on Nevilles and the apostrophe come and go. As to which Neville or Nevilles gave their name to the cross before 1346, no particular individual or episode has yet been identified. As significant landowners, the Nevilles arrived in Co. Durham about 1174 when Geoffrey Neville of Horncastle (Lincolnshire), founder of nearby Tupholme Abbey and descendant of a Norman family, married Emma, daughter and heir of Bertram Bulmer, lord of Brancepeth and Sheriff Hutton, the last representative of a pre-conquest family. At the time of the Battle of Neville's Cross, Brancepeth Castle was the family's chief stronghold, permission for the castellation of Raby manor not being given until later in the century. Often involving himself in local affairs and being employed on royal ones, Ralph Neville in 1346 was one of the three royal Commissioners of Array, raising the army in the north to oppose David of Scotland, when most men and cash were already deployed in France. Why did the name of 'Neville's Cross' stick to the battle rather than the 'Durham' used in some accounts? As already noted, contemporary bards named the Battle from the Neville's Cross and probably more of the population heard the ballads than read the newsletters. Although the prime report of the battle from John Fossor, prior of Durham, to Bishop Hatfield did not mention the words 'Neville's Cross', both Hatfield and the king, with whom he discussed the battle, were familiar with this particular locality and the road north. The king had been in Durham[19] and farther

---

[17] For Neville flamboyance, see *Historiae Dunelmensis Scriptores Tres,* ed. James Raine (SS 9; 1839), p. 74.

[18] For Neville land held of the Bishop of Durham, see ASC, Church Commission (CC) Durham Bishopric records, Coroners accounts (of free rents), *passim.*

[19] For Fossor's letter, see Document a. The 'original' is in London, British Library, MS Cotton Faustina A. VI, fol. 47. When Edward III and Queen Philippa spent Easter 1333 in Durham, the queen was roused in the night from the monastery guest-house and sent to nearby Durham Castle to sleep, the reason given being St Cuthbert's supposed aversion to women. See C. J.

north several times before and would have passed by the Neville's Cross. Ralph Neville's initiative after the battle in replacing the old cross so magnificently would have ensured that locally the victory would continue to have been mentioned in the same breath as the cross with the family's name. No doubt the Neville faction, particularly men who had fought under Neville's command at the battle, fostered reference to the battle as at Neville's Cross for political reasons. Besides, defeat at the site of a cross has an implication of divine (as well as English) retribution on the Scots, further fostered if there were a presentation of Scots trophies to Durham Cathedral after the battle (see above, pp. 57–65). In politics, the moral higher ground is desirable!

The victory and Durham's moment of fame must have seemed a golden time to be talked over a few years later by the survivors of the horrors of the Black Death, a halcyon time appearing the more glorious for its traumatic aftermath. The plague that followed could have made the battle more remembered locally than it otherwise might have been. There may have been local regret that Edward III did not honour Neville and Percy, like his commanders in France, with membership of the new Order of the Garter.

That the Neville's Cross was rebuilt extensively after the battle of 1346 by Ralph Neville is a tradition written down before 1593 in the *Rites of Durham*, a description of Durham Cathedral and its environs as they were before the dissolution of the priory. Apart from the *Rites*, no other independent ascription of Neville's Cross to Ralph Neville has been noticed by the author of this paper. However, there is ample documentary evidence of the cross called Neville's Cross, after (as well as before) the battle and before the tradition was written down in the *Rites*.[20] According to the *Rites*, 'a most notable, famous, and goodly larg Cross of StoneWork [was] erected and sett uppe . . . at the cost and charges of the lord Ralph Nevell', after the Battle of Neville's Cross. A description of the appearance of the stone cross

Stranks, *This Sumptuous Church* (London, 1973), p. 22.

20   *A Description or Breife Declaration of all the Ancient Monuments, Rites, and Customes belonginge or beinge within the Monastical Church of Durham before the Suppression, written in 1593*, ed. James Raine (SS 15; 1842), p. 23; re-edited from the version in the Durham, Dean and Chapter Library, MS C.III.23 as *Rites of Durham, being a Description or Brief Declaration of All the Ancient Monumements, Rites and Customs belonging or being within the Monastical Church of Durham before the Suppression, written 1593*, ed. J. T. Fowler (SS 107; 1900), p. 27. A reconstruction of the cross was drawn from this description and published in W. Hutchinson, *The History and Antiquities of the County Palatine of Durham* (3 vols., Newcastle upon Tyne, 1785–1823), II, 342; but it did not incorporate the original stone socket which survives. For a more credible reconstruction based on surviving crosses, see ill. 12.

with lead reinforcements or embellishments follows. At the top of a stepped plinth, seven steps high, was a socketed stone 1½ yards in height, from which rose the octagonal stalk of the cross another 3½ yards, to an octagonal boss surmounted by a stone carving of Christ on the Cross with Mary and John beside, having a stone canopy over. The arms of Neville were carved on the cross in many places, together with other decoration and prominently the four figures of the evangelists. The words 'the Neville's Cross' can equally well describe the arms of the family, being a saltire, or silver cross of St Andrew on a red ground. The whole impressive monument must have stood 8 or 9 metres high and may have been painted and gilded when new. The *Rites* bewailed the breaking down and defacement of the cross in 1589, but the writer was diplomatic enough not to specify or suggest who was responsible or why. The cross at Cheapside, London, an Eleanor cross, was similarly mutilated in June 1581 as a relic of 'Popish superstition'.[21]

The Battle of Neville's Cross being a close-run victory for the English army, in which Lord Ralph Neville was a chief commander and the Durham monks supposedly active participants through their prayers, the erection of a more elaborate cross could have been justified on several grounds: a thank-offering to God for victory, a way-marker usefully visible from a distance (especially if the top were gilded), a warning proclamation of English might to those on the road to and from Scotland, a celebration of local participation in international affairs, a well-known place for public announcements, or to arrange to meet and sit for business or other meetings, or to have goods left for collection, a usefully well-known landmark, as well as a symbol of the (self) importance of an ambitious family.

During the battle, the author of the *Rites* recounts, a group of monks from Durham Priory, led by Prior John Fossor, had heartened the English army by taking up a position on the battlefield, on the Red Hills later known as 'Maidens Bower'. With them they carried, mounted as a banner, a precious relic, the corporax cloth, which had been in the coffin of St Cuthbert who died in 687. Throughout the battle these monks continued in prayer and were not harmed. After the English victory, the monks set up their own cross at this site. It was of carved wood, 2 yards high, and on subsequent journeys to and from Bearpark the monks stopped to pray there.[22] By making his cross four times as high as the prior's and of stone not wood, Ralph Neville was doubtless making a statement.

21   For the mutilation of the Cheapside cross, see William Andrews, *Old Church Lore* (1891; reprtd. Wakefield, 1975), pp. 142–3.
22   *Description or Breife Declaration*, ed. Raine, p. 25, and *Rites of Durham*, ed. Fowler, p. 25. For investigation of the documentary sources for the tradition of other

Mentions of Neville's Cross continued as usual after the battle. The priory's bursar's account of 1378–9 records the payment of 12*s*. 10*d*. for repair of the road *iuxta Nevilcros* ('by the Neville Cross'). A grant of 1386 again described land called Slateracre as lying beside the priory Cellarer's orchard and on the road leading to *le Nevillcrosse*.[23] In 1505 the tenants of the Borough of Crossgate were ordered not to turn their sheep out to graze in the various lanes, but to put them only on the moor, up by the *Nevilcroce* – or pay a penalty of 40*d*.[24]

Ralph Dalton was Clerk of Works to Bishop Cuthbert Tunstall of Durham for about twenty years (1534–57). Michaelmas 1544 was the date arranged by him for the delivery of two pairs of millstones to be left by the supplier at Neville's Cross. Similarly in 1546, 1548 and 1550, two pairs each year were to be delivered at the Neville's Cross probably some for use in the bishop's mill in Durham City, but certainly some also to be transported onwards to the bishop's mills at Newbottle and Easington.[25]

After 1593 for over a century no other description or picture of the cross is known at present. An undated, mid-eighteenth century drawing, the original of which hangs in Durham University Library on Palace Green shows only the socket of the shaft of the cross surviving on top of an undermined and ruined mound of shallow stones, partly covered with turf, probably the core of the plinth of seven stone steps. Two gentleman are viewing the lonely and prominent cross. Dr Ian Doyle has pointed out the similarity of this drawing in style of garb, gesture etc. to that of Thomas

---

monks watching from the Cathedral tower and singing there later in commemoration, see Brian Crosby, 'The Choral Foundation of Durham Cathedral, *c*.1350–*c*.1650' (unpubl. Ph.D. thesis, University of Durham, 1992), I, 198–203. See also Brian Crosby, 'Singing from the Tower', in the *Annual Report of the Friends of Durham Cathedral*, no.53 (1985–6). That the singing of a *Te Deum* from the tower annually until the Reformation was in commemoration of the victory at the Battle of Neville's Cross was asserted by Surtees, IV, pt.1, p. 5 ('City of Durham Annals'). In 1841 M. A. Richardson, *Local Historians Table Book* (Newcastle, 1841), I, 122, stated that the singing was continued until 1811 when it ceased, but was resumed 29 May 1828. The present writer, arriving in Durham to live and work in 1967, soon heard the tradition that the Cathedral choir sang once a year from the Cathedral tower, at a date which varied to commemorate the English victory at the Battle of Neville's Cross in 1346. The tradition, though interrupted, lives on.

[23] For the 1378–9 repair, see *Account Rolls*, ed. Fowler, p. 588. For the 1386 grant, see ASC, DCDCM, Msc.Ch.1963.

[24] For sheep by Neville's Cross, see ASC, DCDCM, Crossgate Borough Court Book 1498–1524, fol.73r.

[25] For millstones at Neville's Cross: ASC, CC Durham Bishopric 190072, fol. 42v and 190074, fol. 27, and ASC, DCDCM, Msc.Chs. 2926/1 and 2959.

Prelium ad *Nevilli Crucem*
Anno 1340 Templedon 3.

Remains of Neville's Cross

Illustration 6: Neville's Cross in the mid eighteenth century; watercolour by either Thomas Wright, mathematician, architect and astronomer of Byers Green (County Durham), or George Allan, antiquarian and private publisher of Darlington.

Wright's work in his *Louthiana* (1748). The drawing was published in 1857[26] when it was said to be by George Allan, who died in 1800, and that it was in his own interleaved copy of Hutchinson's *Durham*. Allan wrote the caption on the drawing and had owned other manuscripts of Wright's. In about 1778 the cross was sketched from the west, looking past it to Durham Cathedral tower.[27] It shows the mound, the stone socket and a short piece of plain shaft. The mound alone stands higher than the head of the horseman riding by. The artist was Samuel Hieronymous Grimm, a Swiss topographical artist who long enjoyed the patronage of the Reverend Sir William Kaye, who became a canon of Durham Cathedral in 1777. Robert Surtees in 1840[28] (posthumously) printed the description from the

---

[26] For the undermining of the cross mound, see Robert White, 'The Battle of Neville's Cross', *Archaeologia Aeliana*, new series, 1 (1857), p. 283.

[27] These drawings, by Grimm, are in London, British Library, MS Add. 15528.226. He lived 1734–94.

[28] Surtees, IV, pt.2, pp.133–4.

Illustration 7: wood-engraving of Neville's Cross published in the *Gentleman's Magazine* in 1854, based on the watercolour of 1849.

Rites, included a drawing made from the 1593 description, and continued the story of the cross saying that in his time there remained 'only some steps, and a portion of the octagonal shaft' with an 'obliterated milestone' fixed on top, most of the steps being covered with turf.

A sketch by 'E.B.' [Edward Bradley] made in 1849, the original of which hangs also in Durham University Library on Palace Green and a version of which was published in 1854 in the *Gentleman's Magazine,* views the cross from the west, through the toll gate with the tower of Durham Cathedral beyond as Grimm viewed it. This shows most of the mound turf-covered, a little regular stone or brick walling showing at one side at road level.[29] The socket of the cross shaft surmounts it. In the socket is apparently the obliterated milestone mentioned by Surtees a little earlier.

---

[29]   The E. B. drawing, woodcut with accompanying text, is published in *The Gentleman's Magazine,* new series, 42 (1854), opposite p. 356. E. B. was Edward Bradley of University College, Durham University, also known as 'Cuthbert Bede', author of the *Adventures of Mr. Verdant Green* etc. The original drawing was bought by the University Library from Bertram Colgrave in 1957 with others by E. B. I thank Dr. Ian Doyle for this information.

Illustration 8: Neville's Cross: watercolour (dated 1849) by 'E.B.' (Edward Bradley of University College, Durham).

The height of the mound is well above that of the horse and cart passing by on the road.

About 1873, when an area of elegant villas[30] was planned to the north-east side of the cross, it was considered that the cross needed appropriate smartening-up. Money was raised by public subscription and a low wall, stepped to accommodate the lie of the land, was built round the cross. A tall, plain, metal railing was set in the wall, the top ends of some of the railings ending in spear heads. An article by W. Brown in 1891 has a sketch showing it in this state[31] and saying the work had been done about eight years before (in 1883). His description of it was of a 'hotpotch of architectural fragments, encased in brick'. A recent detailed physical examination of the cross has been made recently by Dr G. A. L. Johnson, of the Department of Geology at Durham University. He found that only the socket seems to be original among the fragments surviving in 1996.[32]

---

[30] Plans for villas 1873 are ASC, Small Gift & Deposit 44.
[31] The 1891 sketch is published by W. Brown, 'Neville's Cross', *Ushaw Magazine* 1 (1891) pp.213–24.
[32] Below, pp. 97–101.

Following its 'defacement' in 1589, perhaps as a relic of popery, the cross was not repaired for at least four years and probably not for centuries. It remained ruinous and unattractive, according to sketches, but its history and its position ensured its continued representation on maps, both those printed for wide circulation and those of more local interest which were not printed. What stands out from a study of the place of Neville's Cross in cartography is that both on large wall maps of County Durham and on small maps in the pages of books, the prominence given to Neville's Cross is out of all proportion to its size and illustrates both its commanding position at a high, ancient, crossroads and the persistent fame of the victory and local hero sharing the name. No other Durham city cross is so mapped.

First, some of the printed maps will be considered.[33] Although C. Saxton's map, *Dunelmensis episcopatus,* of 1576 did not mark the cross, then standing to its full height, in 1611 John Speed's map of the *Bishoprick and Citie of Durham* not only marked Neville's Cross (although in the wrong place!) but included two paragraphs of general information in its margin and one of these, with a picture, is about the battle in 1346, then only 265 years before and obviously still talked of. An undated and anonymous map of *c.*1630, *Episcopatus Dunelmensis Vulgo the Bishoprike of Durham,* marked the cross plainly, but placed it, as Speed did, further west within the boundary of Bearpark, where the Scots army spent the night before the battle. Thomas Kitchin in 1763 copied this mistake. Perhaps this placing reflects local memories of that occupation which necessitated extensive repairs at Bearpark *(Beaurepaire),* and also of the fact that the aftermath of the battle (the rout and plunder of those fleeing on foot after the horses had been taken by those fleeing first) took place on the ground between Neville's Cross and Bearpark as archaeological finds suggest. This plundering may have been quite as memorable locally as the main battle nearer Neville's Cross. Prior Fossor's letter (see appendix of this volume) said the battle took place on 'the moor of Bearpark . . . next to our park'. Township boundaries, mapped on the tithe commutation plans of the 1840s but already very old, show the moors next to the park were Crossgate Moor and Framwellgate Moor; however, the name Bearpark Moor appears in some two dozen medieval documents in the muniments of the Dean and Chapter of Durham, on which work is needed to clarify the location. The Neville's Cross being mapped too far to the west could echo a memory of the events named from it taking place further west than where the cross actually stood at the time. In 1768 and 1791 Captain A. Armstrong's map

---

[33] The maps mentioned here are copies in ASC, among the Gibby papers, section H, maps. The originals of most of them, plus others are described in R. M. Turner, *Maps of Durham 1576–1872 in the University Library of Durham, including Some Other Maps of Local Interest : A Catalogue* (Durham, 1954).

placed *Nevils Cross* correctly and marked also *Charlys Cross* and *Phillips Cross* and a cross in Durham market-place. John Cary's plan of the county in 1787, though produced at a small scale to fit on the page of a book with little room for names, still marked the Neville's Cross in preference to other larger nearby landmarks, a policy followed in Hobson's larger county plan of 1840.

These printed and published maps of the whole county showed contemporary communications and settlements throughout the area and portrayed the Neville's Cross in that context. Some unpublished, large-scale, local maps, illustrate this in more detail. There had been briefly a tenement or burgage next to the Neville's Cross on the south side of the road in 1560. Until relatively recently the houses of Crossgate were well down the bank towards the Wear, as the medieval deeds show. The undated mid-eighteenth century sketch shows the cross standing on the unfenced moor with only two small trees and the odd bush in sight. Although possibly not strictly accurate, the artist was obviously stressing the height, loneliness and prominence even of such a ruined cross, on the track over the open moors.

Again no buildings were shown on either side of the road by the cross or anywhere near it on the map of 1770 when the area, Crossgate Moor, was enclosed by Act of Parliament. The award, under the act, lays down the roads north and south-west of Durham City and both are located with reference to the Neville's Cross. The two roads were: northwards Newcastle Lane; and southwards, Stone Bridge Lane, off which the Darlington Lane very soon branched. (The turnpike road for Darlington left Durham from Charley Cross now near the New Inn and that for Newcastle left from the site of the present County Hall roundabout.) That these important routes should be termed 'lanes' indicated the peacefulness of the area then, so different from the present rush of traffic. When Elvet Moor was enclosed in 1773, the Neville's Cross was again used as a landmark. The road east from Stonebridge up the bank was labelled on the enclosure plan as leading to Neville's Cross and Crossgate, rather than to Durham City. Again, when Framwellgate Moor was enclosed in 1809 the road south from Whitesmocks was labelled on the plan as leading to Neville's Cross, a point not actually on the map but well known to all concerned.[34]

The inclosure of moors west of Durham City, by the Neville's Cross, encouraged development of that land once the common rights over those moors had gone. Parallel to this development of land came development of

[34] ASC, DCDCM, Crossgate Moor Inclosure Award and Plan 1770; ASC, DCDCM, Elvet Moor Inclosure Award and Plan 1773; ASC, HC, Framwellgate Moor Inclosure Award and Plans 1809.

road systems near the cross. Turnpike Trusts were set up. In 1793 an Act of Parliament for various turnpikes in County Durham set one up between Crossgate (Durham City) and Wolsingham in Weardale (via Stone Bridge Lane).[35] It is almost certain that it was for this road that the toll bar with its cottage beside the Neville's Cross was erected, thus dating that cottage to *c.* 1793.[36] The toll cottage stood just east of the Neville's Cross on the north side of the road at the corner of what is now St John's Road, then the road to Newcastle. Unfortunately it is also quite likely that this building utilised handy stone from the damaged stepped plinth and other parts of the old cross so conveniently near, as the drawing of 1849 shows, and so contributed to its ruin. As mentioned earlier, sculptured stones built into the walls of the cow byre of the toll house at Neville's Cross had been noticed early in the nineteenth century, and some may have come from the cross.

Although the common land near Neville's Cross had been enclosed in 1770, it was not until after 1856, as the Ordnance Survey plans in successive editions show, that there was any significant housing near the cross. Even in 1895, by which time the toll house (there in 1873) had gone, the houses nearby were well-spaced, substantial Victorian villas in their own large gardens. Many more were planned than were built, as a plan of 1873 shows. However, denser housing was to come. By 1915 the terraced houses just north of the cross between George Street and St John's Road and also down the bank towards Stonebridge, had been built. Durham City had engulfed the moorland cross.

Since about 1953, as residents remember, Neville's Cross has lost also its centuries-old strategic position at a major junction of roads.[37] The main north-south road was straightened and took an alignment a little to the west

---

[35] For the Turnpike Act, see ASC, CC, Durham Bishopric, 344331, 33 Geo.III c.148.

[36] The 25" Ordnance Survey sheet Durham 27/1 (1st edn.), surveyed 1856–7, shows a toll bar clearly across the road from Neville's Cross to Wolsingham in front (south) of the toll cottage, but it also shows a line across the Neville's Cross-to-Newcastle road at the side of the cottage. However, had the cottage been meant to control both roads it would more likely have been erected before the junction where two roads part, not after the junction. Also the road to Newcastle via Neville's Cross was controlled by another toll house less than half a mile away, nearer to Durham City, where Crossgate Peth met Margery Lane. Two toll houses would not be so close together on the same turnpike road.

[37] The cross was still considered a strategic point in the 1939–45 war when the metal plate on it was removed lest any invader be helped by recognising it. For safekeeping the plate was placed in a police house nearby, where a small girl remembered seeing it while on holiday.

Illustration 9: Neville's Cross in 1997, viewed from the east side.

of the cross and a new bridge was put across the nearby railway cutting, the making of which, to its north, had not affected the cross. Now the cross lies off the main north-south route which it had marked for centuries. Once the cross had stood tall on high ground on the open road outside Durham City, now the stump is lost among the roads, houses and gardens of suburban Durham.

As a footnote I mention that in 1889 a small jug of 256 medieval silver coins was found about 400 metres south west of the cross, by the banks of the River Browney.[38] These coins were almost all English and Scottish, dating from the late thirteenth to late fourteenth centuries. As thirty-eight of the coins are of King Robert II of Scotland who became king in 1371, after the David captured at the Battle of Neville's Cross, this hoard is too late to be Scottish plunder hidden before the battle, in which Robert had fought as a young man. However, whoever hid it, about the year 1380, when Edward III's grandson reigned, had the hope of collecting it later and would have committed the place to memory. He or she must, with their back to the curve of the River Browney, have looked up to the top of the open moorland ridge, where high and visible for miles stood the magnificent Neville's Cross.

---

[38] John Evans, 'On a Hoard of Silver Coins found at Neville's Cross, Durham', *Numismatic Chronicle,* 3rd series, 9 (1846–7), pp. 312–21. I am very grateful to the following and other friends and colleagues in several fields with whom I have had fruitful discussions while preparing this paper: David Butler, Ian Doyle, Norman Emery, Niall Hammond, Tony Johnson, Samantha Middleton, Martin Millett, Patrick Mussett, Roger Norris, Michael Prestwich, Lynda and David Rollason, and Martin Snape.

The Neville's Cross Monument:
A Physical and Geological Report

G. A. L. JOHNSON

The monument commemorating the Battle of Neville's Cross lies near the battlefield on the west side of Durham City, close to the junction of the A167 and A690 roads (NZ 26404202). The cross is believed traditionally to have been set up here by Ralph, lord Neville, after the battle, almost certainly on a site where an existing cross already stood (above, pp. 78–84). A description of Lord Neville's cross is given in the *Rites of Durham* and it is further illustrated in Hutchinson's *History* (below, p. 101 and ill. 11) and by Robert Surtees.[1] The illustration follows the written description and is probably an imaginative reconstruction. None of the stones of the contemporary monument fit with those of the illustration. Lord Neville's cross was broken down in 1589 during the Reformation and the present monument seems to have been reconstructed, using some of the original stone, in the seventeenth century. According to James Raine, a mound was formed, containing part of the cross-shaft, not long after the original monument was destroyed and a milestone was added.[2] He also notes that 'six or seven years ago the little mound was effectively secured by stones and soil and so it remains'; the mound must have been given a protective cover of soil about 1820. A lapse of 200 years is quite sufficient time for exposed stonework to decay. Robert Surtees reported on the state of the cross before 1840 as follows: 'There remains only some steps and a portion of the octagonal shaft, on which the heads of the evangelists may still be dimly traced. In this fragment an obliterated milestone is fixed.' Footnote m further notes: 'These last remains were in danger of totally perishing some years ago, but were secured by a mound of turf and stones which covers some of the steps'.[3] This form of protection of rotting masonry was in favour because the western foundations of Durham Cathedral seem to have been treated in a similar way near to this time. An illustration of Neville's Cross produced by R. White in 1857 shows the base of the monument covered by turf on all sides except by the road.[4] On the road side it is

---

[1]   Surtees, IV, 134.
[2]   J. Raine, *St Cuthbert* (Durham, 1828).
[3]   Surtees, IV, 133.
[4]   R. White, 'The Battle of Neville's Cross', *Archaeologia Aeliana* 1 (1857), p. 283.

deeply eroded and shows the interior composed of irregular coursed stones tapering upwards, but with no signs of steps or a thick slab of stone at the top. At the top of the mound the octagonal base to the cross-shaft is clearly recognisable, with the sculptured heads and the square sockets, but the milestone is not shown. About 1883 further repairs were made to the monument and it was surrounded with iron railings. An illustration in the *Ushaw Magazine* in 1891 shows Neville's Cross as a mound covered with turf capped by the recognisable octagonal base to the cross.[5] A vertical milestone, said by William Brown to have been obliterated, is shown set in the base of the cross. (He was assuming that the milestone referred to by Raine and Surtees was still in place.)

In 1903 the monument was moved a short distance to the north to give a wider roadway and subsequently the A167/A690 junction was extensively altered to the plan we know today. Originally Neville's Cross stood jutting into the A690 road near the top of Neville's Cross Bank, but after changes to the roads it now lies near the top of Crossgate Peth. During the 1903 road-works the monument was dismantled and re-erected on a new stone base which kept it at approximately its original surface height (*c.* 100m AOD). The new stone base is level with the ground surface on the north and has stone walls on the east, west and south sides; it has protective iron railings round the top that are derived from those illustrated in 1891. The reconstruction of Neville's Cross in 1903 seems to have faithfully reproduced the mound of coursed sandstone illustrated in the 1857 paper and even the eroded and more vertical face against the road has been preserved. The sandstone blocks of the pedestal and the overlying flagstones appear to be original for the most part, but the plinth of roughly masoned sandstone that lies below the sculptured base of the cross is new. This plinth is a recent addition and probably dates from the 1903 reconstruction. The monument as it stands can be divided into seven sections (illustration 10, opposite) each of which will be described in the following paragraphs.

1) The new base. Rough sandstone walling between masoned coping-stones and quoins. Black iron railings set in the coping-stones on all sides are the late nineteenth-century railings altered and adapted to fit the new sandstone base. Small entrance gate on the north side allows access. This base dates from the 1903 reconstruction.

2) A gently sloping ledge at the top of the new base is formed of small granite cobbles and this forms a surround to the ancient pedestal to the cross. The ledge was formed at the 1903 reconstruction.

---

[5]   W. Brown, 'Neville's Cross', *Ushaw Magazine* 1 (1891), p. 213.

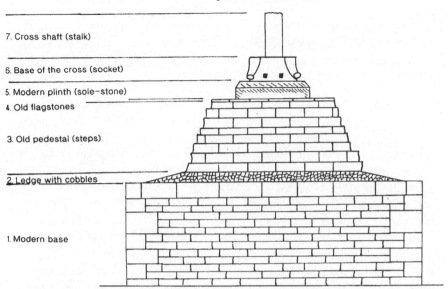

7. Cross shaft (stalk)

6. Base of the cross (socket)

5. Modern plinth (sole–stone)

4. Old flagstones

3. Old pedestal (steps)

2. Ledge with cobbles

1. Modern base

Illustration 10: The Neville's Cross Monument showing the seven parts into which it can be divided. Not to scale and railings omitted.

3) The ancient pedestal or steps to the cross. A pedestal of rough sandstone rubble, eight courses high and gently tapering upwards by each course being set inwards. The sandstone varies in type and size of blocks used. One block of igneous rock, probably from drift, has been incorporated on the east side. Stones are irregular and rounded and look like old re-used stone. Mortar between the stones is thick and repairs using new stone have taken place at various times. The south side of the pedestal, facing the road, has a more vertical face which agrees with the illustration of 1857 and is an original feature preserved in the 1903 reconstruction. The pedestal was dismantled during the 1903 road works and then re-assembled on the new base. The original stones seem to have been used in the re-assembly of the pedestal, possibly with new stone added, but the shape of the present pedestal appears to reproduce the original faithfully.

4) A ledge covered with old flagstones of irregular shape and wide joints pointed with thick mortar forms a cap to the stone pedestal. The original ancient flagstones seem to have been used again at the time of the 1903 reconstruction.

5) Recent sandstone plinth or sole-stone. A plinth of light-coloured micaceous sandstone lies on the flagstone surface. The plinth is in two sections, east and west, each 68 cms x 137 cms and 34 cms thick; they join at the centre. It is roughly masoned with sharp mason marks on the sides.

99

The top edges are chamfered and show very rough chisel marks as if the masons' work was never finished. This is a recent addition to the monument, not shown on either of the nineteenth-century illustrations and probably dates from the reconstruction in 1903.

6) The ancient base or socket to the cross. An octagonal slab of sandstone 1 m x 1 m in plan and 56 cms thick. The sandstone is buff-coloured, medium-grained, micaceous and ferruginous and shows exfoliation with the formation of a thin iron-rich ochreous crust. It is a homogeneous stone and a good freestone that was finely masoned and sculptured. It has the appearance of stone from the Low Main Post, a 10 m thick sandstone band that was quarried in the nearby Browney Valley at Baxter Wood in medieval times. Four of the octagonal faces have a strong weathered boss projecting near to the base. These bosses appear to be the residuals of carved heads projecting from the sides of the slab. Remains of carving can be seen on two of the bosses; the best one is at the north-west corner which in my view is a much eroded bull's head with horns. Between the four faces with bosses there are four faces with two square sockets cut towards the bottom of each. Most of the sockets are empty, but one near the south-east corner contains lead. The sockets seem to have held metal objects fixed in place with lead and most likely they are the holes that once contained the iron and lead fastenings that attached the base of the cross or socket to the underlying plinth or sole-stone as described in the *Rites* (below, p. 104). In support of this, the bottom of some of the sockets is broken as would be expected when the monument was knocked down in 1589. This base to the cross is original and is the most interesting part of the monument.

7) The cross shaft or stalk. An upright shaft, 1 m high and of rectangular section 32 cms x 20 cms. The shaft is set into the sandstone base with lead. The sandstone of the shaft is different to the base. It is a stone that weathers white, a medium to coarse-grained sandstone, micaceous and ferruginous. The shaft is not original. It agrees in size with the shaft identified by W. Brown (see n. 5) as an old milestone set in the base of the cross, but he may have been influenced by references to the milestone by Raine and Surtees early in the nineteenth century. The cross-shaft is not shown on the 1857 illustration by White even though the base of the cross is shown in great detail. Possibly the old milestone was lost between the 1820s and 1850s. The shaft now in the socket might then have been added in about 1883 during restoration when the iron railings were put up. It is clearly shown in William Brown's illustration of 1891. However, the degree of weathering of the sandstone of the existing shaft is greater than of the

plinth or sole-stone which is believed to be under 100 years old. Either the vertical shaft is the old milestone mentioned by Raine and Surtees or an eroded sandstone shaft was added to the monument in 1883.

It is noteworthy that the Charley Cross, opposite the New Inn, has a base of similar stone to the Neville's Cross base. In this cross the shaft is of roughly similar sandstone to the base, but it is not highly weathered and it is set into the base with mortar. Again this shaft may be a replacement and not the original.

Neville's Cross, Durham: A Suggested Reconstruction

MARTIN ROBERTS

On the west side of the City of Durham there was a most notable, famous and goodly large cross of stone work, erected and set up to the honour of God and for the victory had thereof, shortly after the Battle of Durham, in the same place where the battle was fought, called and known by the name of Neville's Cross, which was set up at the cost and charges of the Lord Ralph Neville, being one of the most excellent and chief in the said battle and field

So begins the description of Neville's Cross in the *Rites of Durham*, a late sixteenth-century text, probably the work of a former monk of Durham Priory.[1] It deals primarily with a detailed account of the cathedral church and priory just before the Dissolution, but also offers the most comprehensive description of Neville's Cross, that stood on the western boundary of the city.

In the late eighteenth century a reconstruction of this cross was drawn, possibly for the publication of Hutchinson's history of County Durham,[2] and reappeared in various publications in the following century (illustration 11). The 650th anniversary of the Battle of Neville's Cross in 1996 provided an appropriate occasion to reconsider this reconstruction and the evidence on which it is founded, for it is so historically inaccurate and aesthetically flawed that it seemed that some marginally better informed reconstruction might be made, based on known historical precedents, an examination of local contemporary sculpture and the known wealth and prestige of the Neville family (illustration 12). Any comparison with contemporary crosses must inevitably draw upon the standard work on the subject, Aymer Vallance, *Old Crosses and Lychgates* (London, 1933), an invaluable national source of reference.

The starting point of any reconstruction must be an examination of the cross itself, to identify any original fabric from later repairs and substitutions. Regrettably only the socket appears to be from the original

---

[1]   *Rites of Durham, being a Description or Brief Declaration of All the Ancient Monumements, Rites and Customs belonging or being within the Monastical Church of Durham before the Suppression, written 1593*, ed. J. T. Fowler (SS 107; 1902), p. 27.

[2]   William Hutchinson, *The History and Antiquities of the County Palatine of Durham* (3 vols., Newcastle upon Tyne, 1785–1823), II, 342.

cross. Early engravings offer little more, as there is no record of the cross before its destruction in the late sixteenth century, after which it seems that only the socket was ever incorporated into the rebuilt monument. Very fortunately the detailed description in the *Rites* has survived and this at least enables some idea of the cross's size and design to be formed. In the text that follows, the relevant sections of the cross are assessed against their description in the *Rites* (printed in italics), and in the case of the socket, against what survives of the original fabric of the cross.

STEPS

Which cross had seven steps about it every way, four-squared to the socket that the stalk of the cross did stand in...

The existing 'steps' are constructed of crude rubble stonework, of no practical value as steps for walking up. They appear to be of nineteenth- or early twentieth-century date. Examples more contemporary with medieval crosses range from high steps of over 300 mm (Dundry, Somerset; illustration 13)[3] to more easily climbed examples such as the great Eleanor Cross at Northampton.[4] Such a prestigious cross as Neville's Cross would certainly have had ashlar stone steps and a reasonable rise of at least 250 mm. In the present reconstruction 300 mm has been suggested.

SOLE-STONE

...which socket was made fast to a four-squared broad stone, being the sole, or bottom stone of a large thickness that the socket did stand upon, which is a yard and a half square about every way, which stone was one of the steps and the eighth in number.

The existing stone is not original, being dressed ashlar with a deliberately chipped chamfer on its top edge, a very bad and inappropriate example, probably of nineteenth-century date, of attempting to distress new stonework. The sole-stone has been reconstructed according to the dimensions in the *Rites*, with a thicker depth than the steps, as is also implied in that text. Lewis-holes have been added, reflecting those on the socket.

SOCKET

Which cross had seven steps about it every way, four-squared to the socket that the stalk of the cross did stand in, which socket was made fast to a four-squared broad stone, being the sole, or bottom stone ... Also the said socket was made fast with iron and lead to the sole stone in every side of the corner of the said socket stone, which was three-quarters deep, and a yard and a quarter square about every way...and at every of

---

[3]   Aymer Vallance, *Old Crosses and Lychgates* (London, 1933), p. 70.
[4]   *Ibid.*, frontispiece.

Illustration 11: Neville's Cross: reconstruction in Hutchinson's history of County Durham (1787) (see p. 101, n. 2).

Illustration 12: Neville's Cross: a suggested reconstruction by Martin Roberts.

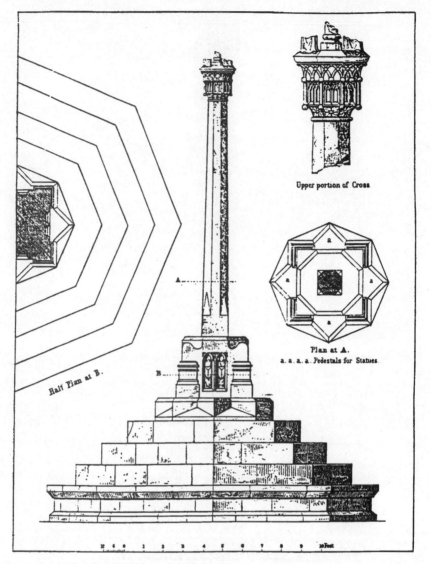

Illustration 13: Churchyard Cross, Dundry, Somerset (from Vallance; see p. 103, n. 3).

the four corners of the said socket below was one of the pictures of the four Evangelists, being Matthew, Mark, Luke and John, very finely set forth and carved in stonemason work.

This is the only stone to survive from the original cross, or at least to have sufficient similarities to the description of the socket stone of the cross to suggest strongly that it is not a replacement. It is cut from local, carboniferous sandstone and has lewis-holes along its bottom edges to facilitate lifting. The width of the stone, at 1010 mm (40") is close to the *Rites's* approximate size of 'a yard and a quarter' (45") and a little less deep, at 560mm (22"), than the 'three-quarters' (27") stated in the text.

The stone has a square base and a chamfered octagonal top, the transition being achieved by four swept faces, which, at their bases at the corners of the stone, have projecting carved work. Two of these can be identified as heads, while the other two have been damaged so that no detail is discernible. Of the two heads, one (north-west corner) is more obviously human in form, the other (south-east corner) having lost its face appears more animal-like with long hair (or a flowing mane?).

The *Rites's* description of 'pictures . . . set forth' seems to fit well with the surviving evidence, and favours the evangelists' heads (or those of their symbolic beasts?) being the sole representation here. The eighteenth-century reconstruction, with full sculptured figures, seems excessive and lacks textual justification (illustration 11). There is also no indication of fixings for such sculptures in the top of the stone, which is plain and without morticing. Such excess was commented on by H. J. S. Swallow in his account of the Battle of Neville's Cross.[5] In a 'Prefatory Note' he opined that the cross 'would probably be more correct if the emblems of the evangelists were substituted for the three figures which appear in the woodcut'.

The centre of the top of the socket is deeply hollowed out for the square base of the original stalk. It now accommodates a plain, rough, stone shaft (probably a milestone or boundary marker), and a packing stone.

STALK

And the stalk of the cross going upward contained in length three yards and a half up to the boss, being eight square about [octagonal], all of one whole piece of stone, from the socket that it did stand in to the boss above, into which boss the said stalk was deeply soldered with lead and solder. And in the midst of the stalk, in every second square, was the Neville cross [saltire] in a scutcheon, being the Lord Neville's arms, finely cut out and wrought in the said stalk of stone. Also the nether end of the stalk was soldered deep in the hole of the socket that it did stand in, with lead and solder.

The present reconstruction shows the height of the stalk as described in the *Rites*. The transition from square base to octagonal shaft is handled in the same way as many similar 'shaft on steps' types of medieval crosses, such as at Cumnor (Berks.), Wicken (Cambs.), Dorchester (Oxon.) and Raglan (Mon.).[6] The great majority of medieval cross-shafts taper gently and this

---

5   H. J. Swallow, *The Battle of Neville's Cross* (1885).
6   Vallance, *Old Crosses*, pp. 61, 62, 63, and 71.

has been suggested here for Neville's Cross too. The carving of the Neville shield on alternate faces of the shaft has been modestly represented here. The text implies cutting into the stone, rather than standing proud, which might have been difficult to achieve in a single stone shaft. 'Finely cut out' has been taken to mean neat and careful work, rather than over-elaborate.

BOSS

And on the height of the said stalk did stand a most large, fine boss of stone, being eight square round about, finely cut and bordered and marvellous curiously wrought. And in every square of the nether side of the boss in the masonwork was the Neville's cross in a scutcheon in one square, and the bull's head, having no scutcheon, in another square; and so contained in every square after the same sort round about the boss.

The precise form and size of the boss is hard to reconstruct accurately. References to 'most large' and 'marvellous curiously wrought' may indicate something quite spectacular. Nevertheless, in the absence of firm descriptive or architectural evidence the present reconstruction has proceeded more modestly, on the basis of known contemporary examples. Medieval crosses with pronounced bosses beneath their crowning sculpture exist, or existed, at St Michael's Mount (Corn.), Keyingham and Hedon (Yorks. ER),[7] the last a finely foliated capital-like design of *c*.1399.[8] At Dundry in Somerset a more ornate (and later?) cross survives with a boss of interlacing arches, beneath the crucifix.[9] The approach taken here has been to interpret the *Rites's* text, so as to accommodate the displays of shield and bulls' heads in simple trefoil-headed panels. The boss rises from the stalk and closes to the crucifix with contemporary mid-fourteenth-century mouldings.[10]

CRUCIFIX

And on the height of the said boss, having a stalk of stone, being a cross standing a little higher than the rest, which was soldered deeply with lead and solder into the hole of the said boss above; whereon was finely cut out and pictured on both sides of the stalk of the said cross the picture of our Saviour Christ, crucified with His arms stretched abroad, His hands nailed to the cross, and his feet being nailed upon the stalk of the said cross below, about a quarter of a yard from above the boss, with the picture of Our Lady, the Blessed Virgin Mary, on the one side of Him, and the picture of St John the Evangelist on the other, most pitifully lamenting and beholding

[7]   *Ibid.*, pp. 71, 72, and 83.
[8]   Nikolaus Pevsner, *Yorkshire: York and The East Riding* (The Buildings of England; Harmondsworth, 1972), p. 246.
[9]   Vallance, *Old Crosses*, p. 70.
[10] H. Forrester, *Medieval Gothic Mouldings* (Chichester 1972), p. 43.

His torments and cruel death, standing both on the height of the said boss. All which pictures were very artificially and curiously wrought altogether, and finely carved out of one whole entire stone, some part thereof (being) through carved work, both on the east side and the west side of the said cross, with a cover of stone likewise over their head, being all most finely and curiously wrought together out of the said whole stone, which cover of stone was covered all over very finely with lead.

This is the climax, indeed the whole *raison d'être*, of the cross, and given the very detailed description that survives, care is needed in suggesting a reconstruction. A number of points need airing: the sculpture's position relative to the boss, its two-directional quality and the extent and form of the carving. The *Rites* seems to suggest that the main cross rises as a stalk from the top of the boss, in much the same manner as the main cross stalk sits in the socket. The mourners are fixed into the top of the boss, yet still part of the same single carved stone. This implies a degree of separation between the boss and crucifix, rather similar to the crucifixes at Somersby (Lincs.), Tyberton and Madely (Herefords.) (illustrations 14 and 15).[11] The cross at Dundry (Somerset), referred to above has a relationship between crucifix, mourners and boss that fits the *Rites's* description reasonably well, though mourners are detached there, but this general approach has been adopted for the reconstruction.

The alternative form of crucifix known is that in which the crucifix rises from the boss as a stone block, with no sense of a detached stalk. The type is usually panelled on two or four principal faces, with relatively low relief sculpture set under arched heads, framed by buttresses and flanked by pinnacles. The cross at Pocklington (Yorks. ER) is a good example.[12] This type seems to be a later form and does not accord as well with the *Rites's* description as does the Dundry detached type. The crucifix clearly had two faces, east and west, presumably with figures carved back to back. There is also 'through carved work' implying that the carved group was not monolithic in character, but had some separation between, perhaps, mourners and the cross-base. This description reinforces the detached approach adopted in the present reconstruction.

There was a 'cover of stone over their head', which has been interpreted in the reconstruction as a roof-like design, capable of taking the lead referred to. The excellent examples at Tyberton and Madeley (Herefords.), mentioned above, provide a possible design.

* * * * *

---

[11]   Vallance, *Old Crosses*, pp. 73 and 82–3.
[12]   *Ibid.*, p. 87.

Illustration 14: Cross at Tyberton, Herefordshire.

This paper has attempted to reconstruct the imposing medieval Neville's Cross on the basis of the surviving material, a detailed historical description and comparison with similar crosses nationally. It is a venture fraught with difficulties, not least because the surviving fabric is so limited and the availability of contemporary local examples non-existent. An examination of contemporary sculpture in Durham, or in the Nevilles' patronage, may offer some further, but limited, help. The question of the Nevilles' power of patronage raises the problem of architectural and sculptural excellence, raised in considering the boss (see above). The Neville Screen, begun in 1372 and consecrated in 1380,[13] was dedicated to the memory of Ralph Neville, hero of the battle, who died in 1368. It was most certainly the product of the royal works in London, under the direction of one of the greatest master masons of their day, either William Ramsay or Henry Yevele. The screen was prefabricated in London, carved out of Caen stone

[13] Christopher Wilson, 'The Neville Screen', in *Medieval Art and Architecture in Durham Cathedral* (The British Archaeological Association Conference Transactions for 1977; Leeds, 1980), p. 90.

Illustration 15: Cross at Madeley, Herefordshire.

from Normandy, and shipped up to Newcastle, piece by piece. It is widely regarded as one of the finest pieces of medieval sculpture anywhere in the country. In short the Nevilles were well capable of commissioning the best sculpture from the best designers and workshops at considerable expense. Against this background it should be noted that the present reconstruction has followed a more cautious path than to suggest that the Neville's Cross was so magnificent that it outstripped all other medieval crosses before it, in the excellence of its design and execution. It may well have been as fine as the screen that followed it (though the modest evidence of the socket argues against this).

Contemporary village and church parallels are inevitably more local in origin and little from the north-east of England has survived. Yet with all these constraints and conditions, it is hoped that the reconstruction suggested here may take us a little nearer to an accurate representation of the cross, which stands as the sole reminder of the Battle of Neville's Cross in 1346.

111

The Military Archery at Neville's Cross, 1346

ROBERT HARDY

On 26 August 1346, Edward III's army of English men-at-arms and archers and Welsh archers and spearmen crushed the vastly superior forces of Philip of France, on the low ridge and valley that runs between Crécy-en-Ponthieu and Wadicourt. The victory was a great shock to the French. The thousands of longbowmen of Edward's army, preserving perfect discipline and shooting arrows 'so thickly and evenly that they fell like snow',[1] outranged the mercenary crossbowmen sent forward by the French to open their attack, and then shot down fifteen or sixteen separate cavalry charges, or so disorganised them that, though hard-pressed, the English men-at-arms, fighting on foot, were able to hold their positions. France reeled; King Philip, wounded in the face by an arrow, narrowly escaped and set about persuading his young Scottish ally, King David, to invade England and provide a diversion.

The details of the Scottish attack, the sacking of Lanercost and so forth, and the advance towards Durham, are dealt with earlier in this volume. Edward of England, with rare strategic foresight, had provided for just such a contingency, and was able to field a capable army to oppose the invasion. It seems as if this army, under the command of Henry Percy, Ralph Neville, the archbishop of York, Lord Mowbray and Thomas of Rokeby, was comparable to the small force with which Henry V, sixty-nine years later, faced the massive French army at Agincourt. It is likely the total English force at Neville's Cross was about 6,000 strong, though the proportion of men-at-arms to archers was probably higher than the Agincourt force which numbered 1,000 men-at-arms and 5,000 archers.

The contemporary *Anonimalle Chronicle* of St Mary's Abbey at York speaks of an army of over 10,000 archers and men-at-arms,[2] and equally contemporary lists suggest a number of just over 3,000 mounted archers.[3] The speed with which the English responded to the Scottish threat rather suggests that at least the greater part of the archer force had been swift-moving, so I am inclined to think that between 3,000 and 4,000 archers out of a total force of 10,000 represents the proportion fielded at

---

[1] *Froissart Chronicles,* ed. G. Brereton (Harmondsworth 1968), p. 88.

[2] Document d.

[3] PRO E101/25/10; document i.

Neville's Cross. Thus, if the total was more like 6,000, 2,000 archers would seem a likely proportion, most of them mounted. The question is: how effective were they, and what could they achieve with their weapons in 1346?

David of Scotland thought the main strength of the English was across the Channel. Edward III, foreseeing the threat, had provided against it, and though he probably took the cream of both English and Welsh bowmen with him, he certainly left behind a force of archers to be reckoned with.

According to a report of the battle written in a letter by one Thomas Sampson, and of which copies can be seen in the Bodleian Library, Oxford, 'twice', once battle was joined, 'the archers were driven back' (*deux fois se retrairerent les archers e communes de nostre partie, mais nos gents d'armes se combatierent e se continuerent durment bien tantq les arches e communes reassemblerent*). We are offered a picture of an archer force which perhaps lacked both the numbers and the solid cohesion of the Crécy bowmen, but which nevertheless was sufficiently well-ordered and disciplined to get themselves back into action after a reverse.[4]

Before offering a little research into the effectiveness of these archers' weapons, a short footnote: why, at a Durham battle was the warlike Thomas Hatfield, bishop of Durham, not in the command structure? He was, in fact, with Edward's army in France, and when during the Battle of Crécy the sixteen-year old Prince Edward of Wales in the vanguard, or English right wing, was hard pressed by the French, those about the prince sent for help to his father, who held a large reserve behind the immediate battle-lines. The king sent the famous answer back 'let the boy win his spurs',[5] but did allow the Bishop of Durham, with twenty knights, to go to his son's assistance.

In my book *Longbow: A Social and Military History*, first published in 1976, I wrote: 'I believe we cannot be far wrong if we say that by the reign of Edward III his archers would have used longbows of 80 *lb* up to 160 *lb* draw-weight, achieving ranges up to 300 yards.'[6] When the archery world in general laughed at my claim, I argued that my guesswork was based on the sort of bow-strength that would best have suited the one surviving medieval arrow we then knew of, found in Westminster Abbey in 1878, which I and my team had measured for 'spine', or stiffness, and weight, allowing for shrinkage and desiccation. The results of those measurements suggested very heavy bows – heavy, that is, to modern longbow archers who seldom use bows stronger than 60–65 *lbs* draw-weight.

---

4   Document b.
5   *Froissart Chronicles*, p. 92.
6   3rd edn (Sparkford, 1992), p. 54.

Indeed, one was working in the dark until in 1979 unexpected, almost unbelievable, light began to flood the obscurity. It will be remembered that the wreck of the *Mary Rose*, located in the 1830s, then lost because of inaccurate charting, had been re-discovered in the 1960s.[7] The ship, Henry VIII's vice-admiral, and the pride of his fleet had sunk with all hands in full view both of the king and his troops at Southsea, and of a large French invasion fleet in the Solent in the summer of 1545. In 1979 I was telephoned by Dr Margaret Rule, Archaeological Director of the *Mary Rose* Trust. On her desk, among the many books on shipbuilding, ship rigging, ship armament and so on, was a copy of *Longbow*. Dr Rule had said, 'Try and get hold of this Robert Hardy.' I raced down to Portsmouth with Professor Peter Pratt and Professor John Levy; the first, Professor of Crystal Physics at the Imperial College of Science and Technology with whom I had been working on longbow research for some time; the second, Professor of Wood Science, also at Imperial College, who was already consultant to the Trust on the ship's timbers. The chief diver had surfaced the day before our arrival with a long, rather knobbly stave from the wreck site and Dr Rule, identifying it as a longbow, one of the 250 listed in the ship's armaments roll, which is to be seen in Magdalene College, Cambridge, wanted longbow people to examine it. Was it a bow, or, as some thought, a pikestaff? It was a bow, a great big Tudor war-bow, blackened from long immersion and covered in oyster spat and other underwater accretions. Our excitement was intense. It was the first truly authenticatable military bow of such an early date, and it was obviously of a hefty weight. The roughness of its timber hardly surprised us, because it is hard to find long clean staves of yew-wood without pins and knots, and this weapon was all but seven feet long. Then came another, and another, and in no long time a whole bow-box full of bows was brought up to the deck of *Sleipnir*, the support vessel moored permanently over the wreck-site. Another full box followed, and box by box, thousands of arrows.

The world knows that the *Mary Rose*, finally emptied of all her treasures, was raised to the surface in 1982, and eventually put on public view in a new museum in Portsmouth harbour, beside HMS *Victory*, and not many yards from where, as the first purpose-built Tudor warship, her keel was laid in 1509.

The wealth of artefacts raised from the wreck, and now to be seen in the museum, is beyond compare. For our purposes we must turn aside from the stern beauty of the guns, the intimacy of the thumb-print in the ointment box found in the barber-surgeon's cabin, the golden glow of the 'angel' coins, and concentrate on the 138 complete longbows, the many broken pieces of other bows, and the thousands of arrows that had been

[7]   Margaret Rule, *The Mary Rose* (London, 1982), *passim*.

issued to the archers aboard *Mary Rose* in 1545 and which now provide us with irrefutable proof of the skill of Tudor bowyers and fletchers, the potential power of the weapons and the strength and constant practice that were needed from the archers to make them formidable weapons of war.

As the slow processes of conservation began and the bow timbers began drying out, it became apparent that we were dealing with big weapons, well beyond the capabilities of most archers nowadays, and with fully completed bows of the finest quality imaginable, none as knobbly as that very first bow raised.

It was evident that all the bows were made of fine-grained yew timber, cut radially from logs across the sapwood and heartwood boundary, which allows the highly tensile sapwood to remain on the back, or convex side, of the drawn bow, lying against its own heartwood towards the centre of the log, which forms the belly or concave side of the bow, and which is probably the timber with the best resistance to compression known to man. Yew timber, if so cut and used, offers a natural spring, and no other timber has been found to surpass its combination of tensility and strength.

When the bows from the chests were still wet, they had almost the appearance of new wood, though it was only after drying that the pale sapwood took on the true colour that one sees today in a yew bow made fifty or a hundred years ago. The deep reddish brown of the belly lightened as the timber dried through the months, and later gentle oiling and waxing restored to them something of their youthful look. It was possible from the detailed examination of broken fragments to establish that there was a degree of cell degradation in the timber surfaces, but whether there was vital degradation in the many complete bows could only be revealed by testing their elasticity and strength. It was also clear from the narrowness of the growth rings, in some cases reaching over 100 to the inch that the timber was extremely slowly grown. This suggested two things: strength and a foreign provenance; and the average radius of the growth rings suggested that the bowmakers had chosen grown timber of more than eight inches diameter.

During the long months of cleaning and drying, each bow was examined, and preliminary measurements were taken. A complicated system of description and identification was begun to record the idiosyncrasies of each weapon. In many instances, among the best preserved, the extraordinary skill and confidence of the bowyers with their draw-knives, or 'floats', were plain to see, even to feel, like delicate fluting on a glass stem. So sure were the bowmakers of their skills and of their timber that they clearly felt no need to work out those last straight marks of manufacture, as we would now.

The bows were found variously about the ship, on the weather deck, in which number must be included those that fell into the ship from the bow and stern castles, either on impact with the sea bottom or during later disintegration of the castles; in the gun deck, and in the orlop. In one chest were forty-eight bows, in the other thirty-six, almost all in miraculously fine condition after 437 years' immersion. The rapid inflow of silt accounts for the good state of preservation, which is far better than would have been the case if the bows had been preserved in air, since much of the natural make-up of the timber was sealed in anaerobic conditions.

It was noticed at once that every bow, no matter what condition it was in otherwise, as long as one or both tips remained, showed at the tips a plain differentiation of colour for some 5 cms. This was clear evidence that the tips had originally been covered by an applied nock of some kind. Since horn is and was the most usual material for such applied nocks, and since horn has been proved to perish fairly rapidly in the conditions of the Solent silt, it can safely be assumed that the nocks were of horn. This is borne out by the fact that of the thousands of arrows recovered, having a slot at the nock end which runs down towards the fletching and which would originally have taken a horn sliver for the purpose of strengthening the force-absorbing end of the arrow, only one or two still have the horn in place. Those few only remain as a result of being protected, for instance by a coil of tarred rope, from the effects of micro-biological and seawater decay. It is also notable that among all the *Mary Rose* finds, no horn buttons have survived, no horn panels for lanthorns, no horn handles, though it is obvious that there had been many such articles in 1545.

Since writing that paragraph, which remains true, the exception proving the rule has arisen. In July 1997, Maggie Richards, Research Assistant at the *Mary Rose* Trust, wrote me a letter, from which I quote:

> I thought that you would be interested in a recent *Mary Rose* find (MR97A0003). It is a horn nock for a longbow! Last Thursday, I was excavating a concretion containing human bones, when I came across the nock. Immediately I knew it was a longbow tip; but due to its size and the depth of the notch for the bow string, I was also convinced that it was covered with a horn nock. I am glad to say that my initial instincts have proved correct, Dr Mark Jones has today confirmed that it is horn, and is investigating the best method for conservation. I have enclosed a 1:1 drawing for your records.
>
> The concretion was recovered from the Upper Deck sector 5. The unfortunate individual whose bones were caught in the concretion may have been an archer. Besides the longbow nock, a small fragment of arrow was also found. The concretion also contained what could possibly be very degraded body armour. I have searched the database for a longbow from U5 with its tip missing, but have had no success.

I hope this information is of interest; it is satisfying to have positive evidence for the attachment of horn longbow rocks, in addition to the discolouration of the bow tips. This new piece of evidence surely will convince any remaining 'doubters' that the *Mary Rose* bows are not bowstaves, but are indeed bows ready for use as you state in your book *Longbow*.

In the opinion of the Consultants these *Mary Rose* longbows, whether found at action stations or in boxes in the orlop, were finished weapons ready for use. It might seem unnecessary to make such an obvious claim, but it is necessary because within the archery world a good deal has been said and written expressing the view that the *Mary Rose* longbows are not bows, but bowstaves, unfinished and not ready for use. Apart from the very oddity of the idea that a ship of war, in time of war and actually in action against the enemy, should put to sea for action with no longbows but a large number of unfinished staves, there is the massive evidence of the bows themselves. What started the hare of this nonsense was our first published suggestion of the draw-weights of these bows. It was hard to believe them ourselves. Few believed us when we came up with the first massive weights, arguing that the *Mary Rose* bows ran from about 100 *lb* drawweight at 30 inches to 180 *lb*. These estimates were obtained from a computer model invented by Dr Bob Kooi of Gröningen University to whom we supplied detailed measurements and he in turn came up with the bows' optimum and original strengths. Many said these weights were impossible, and that therefore the bows must be unfinished, carrying more timber and hence more weight than they would when completed. That they are completed is now self-evident.

By this time we ourselves had completed three or four copies of *Mary Rose* bows, or rather 'approximations' (since in following the dictates of individual staves, a true copy can never be achieved) of which we knew all the relevant details. When the vital statistics of these weapons were fed into the Kooi computer their draw-weights came out with absolute accuracy, so we had to believe them.

All the bows were made from yew timber, each from a single, unjointed, unpieced stave. The quality of the timber, its density, the extreme fineness of the grain in most cases, suggested that we were dealing with imported staves of a straighter and finer quality than can readily be found in the soft climates of the British Isles. That most of it was imported from the Continent there is small doubt, and several documents from Henry VIII's reign record such imports either through Venice by the Doge's special permission or from elsewhere by special mandate of the Emperor Maximilian.[8] Such timber would be gathered from those parts of

---

[8]   *Letters and Papers Foreign and Domestic of the reign of Henry VIII, 1509-13*, p. 529.

Europe – Spain, when she was not our enemy, Italy, Austria, Poland – where the yew grew high and fine-grained, and where for centuries timber had been felled and split into staves to supply our military needs.[9] Henry VIII was a great encourager of the military use of the longbow, just as he keenly pursued the development of gunpowder artillery. He sent his agents into Europe to choose the finest yew timber, selecting at a time thousands of the best staves which were then stamped with the Rose and Crown for export to England. The orders were almost always large – one part-order was for 40,000 staves to be sent to England through Venice[10] – and the names exist of five bowyers who made up 600 of this particular batch of staves into finished bows, for which they were paid altogether £200 13s. 4d. at a time when a master carpenter was paid 4d. a day and beef was about 2d. a pound.

After long and frequent examination we came to the conclusion that the bows showed exactly what today's longbows show in the way of age and use. Those in regular use exhibit a slight or a marked 'string-follow', that is they remain curved towards the belly, or 'de-flexed'; one of the deck bows was certainly in use when the ship foundered and the string somehow survived long enough to set the bow in the braced position for good. Others lie almost straight; but a majority of the boxed bows show a 'reflex', a bend towards the back, away from the natural bow shape. The probable reasons for this curvature are either natural, the bowyers selecting timber with a natural bend towards the back, or the fact that when bowstaves are split from recently cut logs they will tend to reflex themselves. The result in either case is just what the bowyers were after, timber that would maintain optimum straightness after much use, which means a longer and faster return of the limbs from full-draw to the braced position at which the arrow quits the string. The faster that return, the greater the bow's ability to cast an arrow. Since most of the boxed bows appear to be new bows, they were probably intended for land service not naval use.

The *Mary Rose* bows are handle-less. There are no indications of any binding being put on them, and it must be assumed they had none. The approximate position of the 'arrow-pass' is just above the handle position (for even without a marked handle section, there is of course still a handle position), and it is in very many cases indicated on the *Mary Rose* bows by incised, pricked, and in some cases stamped, marks.

The marks consist mainly of groups of incised dots, as if made with a chisel corner (perhaps a float-blade corner) arranged in pairs, threes,

---

Also *ibid.*, p. 566 (4 September 1510), and *Calendar of State Papers, Venetian*, II, 78 (Licence passed 5 May 1510 for 40,000 longbows).

9   Roger Ascham, *Toxophilus, 1545*, ed. Edward Arber (London, 1902).

10   *Letters and Papers Foreign and Domestic, Henry VIII*, p. 757 (see above, n. 8).

crosses, or little tree-like groups. There is a variety of circular marks: plain circles, circles with a cross, segmented circles, some apparently made with dividers, one or two possibly with a tubular stamp. There are variations on the cross: plain, and with dots in various arrangements. There are other linear marks, often in association with dots, sometimes whole clusters of pinpricks up to thirty or more in number. In general there seems a difference between the heavy marks which suggest a maker's advice or identification, and rather more random markings which could be personal additions. But those bows which are not marked at all, some fifth of the total, do not seem to be generally inferior, or different from the marked bows.

Though it is hard to detect a standard in these marks, it is certain there was hardly a standard bow; yew does not yield to a standard; there are not two dozen bows at exactly 100 *lb* and two dozen at exactly 110 *lb* and so forth. There are more standard arrows at predictable lengths; the bow by its nature is personal and unique, first in the timber, then in the bowyer's hands, then in the hands of the archer.

There is a painting in the manuscript collection of Christ Church, Oxford, an illumination of 1326, showing a castle defended by two women, one using a massive crossbow, the other an equally massive longbow. The moral of that is: training can make nearly all things possible. Does anything lead us to suppose that bows of the weights represented by the *Mary Rose* collection would be unusable? The answer must be no. If they were unusable they would not be there. So, if we admit them usable, what is there to suggest that the men who used them were specially selected, specially trained? The answer is: a very great deal. Those skeletons found in the *Mary Rose* which can undoubtedly be linked with archery tackle, and can be presumed to have been those of archers, belonged to large men, six-footers or so, and described by the Senior Consultant Anthropologist to the Trust who examined them as 'huge ... not necessarily tall, but massively boned'. The shipboard location of skeletons representing the highest percentage of bone-changes attributable to the use of heavy bows occurs in the areas most associated with archery equipment. Even with the lighter bows we use for sport today it is in the shoulders, the upper arm and the elbows that things tend to go wrong. The lengths of the bows, from just over 6 feet to just under 7 feet suggest men of some 5 feet 7 inches to over 6 feet, and the arrow measurements, with average draw-lengths of 30 inches confirm these as likely proportions.[11]

Increasingly today there are to be found those who are teaching themselves to master bows of such great weights. I know of, and benefit

[11] The arrow-lengths range from 28 inches to 34 inches. See the *Mary Rose* full report of finds, yet to be published.

from the skills of, young archers who can handle weights well over 100 *lbs*, as well as those who have trained themselves to shoot, with reliable accuracy, twenty and more arrows in a minute. Turn those few into thousands and one begins to get a genuine idea of the formidable power of our archer corps throughout the long years of its military ascendancy. What sort of men could use the *Mary Rose* bows? Young, fit men in constant practice chosen for well-paid military service from a nation to which the shooting of longbows had been second nature for 250 years at least; men who by and large came from intensive rural labour, whose bodies, and stamina were certainly formidable in comparison with average male bodily strengths today.

By Henry VIII's reign, military archery was in decline. Can we infer that in these heavy bows rescued from the Solent we have the sort of weapons that were used at Bosworth, at Towton, at Agincourt, Poitiers, and at Crécy and Neville's Cross 200 years before the *Mary Rose* archers sailed out of Portsmouth? I see no reason why we cannot be confident of that. If decline in the use of the weapon is going to change anything in the weapon itself, it will tend surely to diminish the strength of it, not increase it. We cannot but believe we now have available to see and to study nearly 140 bows that represent the great period of military archery. The *Mary Rose* bows were part of the equipment of the army of Henry VIII, himself a fine longbowman, who went to great lengths to procure the finest timber for his archers; he was also an innovator in the use and development of artillery. Within those terms of reference it seems to me unlikely either that he was demanding from his bowyers the making or from his archers the use of either heavier, or lighter bows than were previously in general use. Because of the growth of artillery we might expect a downturn in the strength of bows, just as there is a lowering of the proportion of archers to other arms in his army recruitment. It cannot be that there is a drop in bow strengths, because if there is, from what weights, drawable by man, can bows of 180 *lb* draw-weight have diminished? Can we suppose that he demanded greater weights, greater feats than he inherited from the past of military archery? When it was becoming increasingly difficult to recruit and train archers, it is scarcely credible that the use of the weapon itself should have been put beyond average trained practitioners. I see no reason to suppose these bows we have from 1545 differ in general from the military weapons of the Hundred Years' War. Therefore I believe we can argue usage and tactics during these wars from the evidence of the weapons that we have recovered from the Solent.

We are now beginning to know from practical experiments (which are by no means complete) that effective bow range can exceed 300 yards, though not I think by much. It depends on the purpose of long-range shooting, and the weights and designs of arrows shot. So let us take 300 yards as the length at which the first fall of arrows can begin to be effective, and let us take 2.8–3.3 *oz* (80–95 gms) as the sort of all-up arrow weights that would be shot those distances; arrows with armour-piercing bodkin heads or small barbed heads. We now know from practical tests that it not only takes a very powerful bow to propel such arrows, but that once shot from a strong bow such heavy arrows fly long and well and strike with great impact. Given the proportion of archers to men-at-arms at Agincourt, or Crécy, what would the commanders have done? Deployed them to best advantage, I take to be the answer. At Agincourt the English and French engaged on a front of approximately 1,000 yards; at Crécy where larger numbers were involved, and again from the lie of the land, which because of terracing would have allowed for a very light defence of the centre, the whole front seems likely to have been almost a mile. If, as is sometimes argued, the archers were placed only on the wings of the entire battle array, then there was at Agincourt at least 300 yards of front which the French could attack, unswept by the fall of arrows; at Crécy there was something like 1,100 yards. Does that make any sort of sense? We are left with the only sensible proposition: that each 'battle' in the whole army line-up, whether it was double or triple, had its own archer wings, so deployed as comfortably to cover the front from the left of the rearguard to the right of the vanguard. The fact that I believe archers were often placed in front of the whole line during the early stages of attack, and that drills existed for them to move sideways among their fellows on the wings, or back behind the men-at-arms to re-deploy as needed, will probably not greatly influence those who force contemporary accounts to back their beliefs that the vastly effective English archer forces were only deployed on the extreme wings of the entire battle line, and thus unable to cover the centre of the field of action. Alas, there are no drill-books. We still do not know quite how the archers stood, or moved in their formations, how orders were given for general marshalling, or for companies in the roar and din of battle, but we are pushed towards various common-sense conclusions, and guided by – dare I repeat Alfred Burne's extremely sensible phrase 'inherent military probability'?

Let us look at the man himself – the archer of the Hundred Years' War. After Crécy, the great shocks the French had to face were that their chivalry could be shot down, and that crossbows were outranged by longbows. The crossbow of the time, with wooden or composite limbs, was probably not capable of much more than 200 yards. The Genoese could have had the 6,000 that some chroniclers attribute to them,[12] and still the battle would have been no different.

[12]   Giovanni Villani (d. 1348), *Cronica : con le continuazioni di Matteo e Filippo* (Turin,

When two such armies met again ten years later at Poitiers the crossbows on the French side appear to have done considerable damage, but were certainly not decisive.[13] They would remain in military use, and the invention of the steel bow would greatly improve their range and penetration, and turn them into a siege weapon or a marksman's bow of high value. In 1901 a 400-year-old crossbow was shot by Sir Ralph Payne-Gallwey, reaching nearly 400 yards.[14] By the time of Agincourt there is no doubt that crossbows could reach something like 400 yards, and probably outrange longbows, but with their increase in power came complications in loading, and the hopeless inequality of shooting speed was increased. Tests today, as well as the evidence of history, suggest that a crossbow could only be spanned and shot twice in a minute, while a skilled longbowman can and no doubt could loose up to 20 aimed arrows in the same time.

There is a footnote worth adding to the question of military archery for the armies of the late middle ages. By the time the rifle had reached a speed of fire that equalled the speed of shooting of longbowmen nearly 600 years earlier, most British riflemen carried 150 rounds each in their belts and pouches. There would be a further 100 rounds per man in the ammunition trains for each regiment, another 50 rounds each in Brigade ammunition columns, 50 more in Divisional columns, and a further 200 each in the base ammunition park and in reserve columns. The total for an infantry rifleman was thus 550 rounds. The long history of the handgun, which replaced the bow, shows that as the weapon became more efficient and capable of faster fire so the number of rounds provided for each soldier increased. In 1338 the king's 'artiller' was Nicholas Corand, who was ordered at one time to buy 1,000 bows and 4,000 sheaves of arrows, to make what he could not buy, and despatch them with all haste to John de Flete, keeper of the king's armour.[15] The proportion of arrows to bows in this instance is either 96 to 1 or 120 to 1 depending upon whether the sheaves in 1338 contained 24 or 30 arrows each. Here anyway is an indication that an archer on campaign could count on 100 shafts, more or less, presumably replenished as often as necessary and possible. I find it impossible to believe that commanders of the calibre of Edward III and Henry V, and the rest, wasted the enormous potential of their infantry

1979); *Froissart Chronicles*, p. 88, speaks of 15,000 Genoese, surely much too high. Their commanders were Odono Doria and Carlo Grimaldi.

[13] *Chronicon Galfridi le Baker de Swynbroke*, ed. E. M. Thompson (Oxford, 1889), pp. 147–8.

[14] Sir R. Payne-Gallwey, Bt, *Crossbow: Mediaeval and Modern, Military and Sporting*, 2nd edn (London, 1958), p. 21.

[15] *CPR 1338–40*, pp. 124–5.

weapon by failing to supply their archers with enough arrows. What those archers achieved proves that they had, apart from exceptional instances, enough arrows.

In the wake of the victories at Crécy and Neville's Cross, Edward III had no great difficulty in raising men and money for his new army to besiege Calais and at the same time hold off any French attempts to attack him or relieve the town. The roll of his forces at Calais exists. In 1347 he had cavalry numbering 5,340 and foot totalling 26,963. Of these, 20,076 were archers, 4,025 of them mounted.[16] That vast host of 32,303 men must have been the largest English army ever to take the field until that time, and the figures are trustworthy.

Within the year the Black Death had begun to ravage Europe and the British Isles, killing perhaps a third of the population before it died out, and it was a long time before such armies could be equalled again. But whatever the size of the armies, from now the proportion of longbowmen in them was always as high as could be achieved. Proportions of 3, 4, 5 to 1 were common and sometimes reached as high as 20 to 1. To quite a substantial degree the archer could be seen as replacing the man-at-arms.

The fourteenth century, in the situation of hostility between France and England, was witnessing the emergence of a kind of national consciousness in England, certainly an anti-French and anti-Scots feeling in general, in which many Welshmen joined. In this context I would refer anyone to Professor Prestwich's *The Three Edwards*[17] where he not only points out how in the century before Neville's Cross, an interdependent method of army organisation had been achieved, but goes on to give good reason for English and Welsh apprehension of Scottish fighting methods. Speaking of Falkirk (1298) he says:

> Now a properly combined force could be organised, with the archers providing the offensive fire-power and the men-at-arms the muscle for hand to hand conflict. By the 1330s a standard battle formation had been developed, with each battalion of dismounted men-at-arms flanked by wings of archers.

He continues:

> It was said that James Douglas, who died in 1330, had such a respect for the English longbow that he either cut off the right hand or gouged out the right eye of any English archer he captured. A legal record of

---

[16] G. Wrottesley, *Crécy and Calais* (1989), pp. 191–204. For a recent discussion of the size of 1346–7 army, see A. Ayton, 'The English Army and the Normandy Campaign of 1346', in *England and Normandy in the Middle Ages*, ed. D. Bates and A. Curry (1994), pp. 253–68.

[17] Michael Prestwich, *The Three Edwards: War and State in England 1272–1377*, 2nd edn (London, 1993), p. 70 and *passim*.

Edward II's time describes three sorts of bow: one of these 'the classic longbow', was two ells in length, and fired a *clotharrow* a yard long. ... These bows were made of imported Spanish yew, but native yew was also used... It is likely that the heaviest bows had a range of up to 400 yards, though real accuracy was unlikely beyond 200. A rate of fire of ten flights a minute was possible; a constantly reiterated simile of fourteenth-century chroniclers is that arrows fell like snow on the battlefield; but unlike snow, arrows produced a terrifying noise, bewildering men and panicking horses. At Dupplin Moor and Halidon Hill the archers were able to decimate the Scottish troops before they even approached close to the English positions, so anticipating the later successes of Crécy and Poitiers.

And of course, Neville's Cross.

It has been said that those who fought with the two Edwards at Crécy comprised an army that was part-Norman, part-Saxon, Angevin and Celtic, but which in some way thought of itself as the army of England.[18] Care and effort were taken to explain to people in general, often from the pulpit, often in the market place, what was happening, how the war was going, why the French or the Scots were liable to invade, and why England must go to war in France.[19]

The war allowed the king to take advantage of the desires of men outlawed for many sorts of crime to regain freedom within the law. In 1339 and 1340, 850 charters of pardon were granted to men who had served as soldiers or sailors. In the year of Crécy several hundred more were granted, both for service in Scotland in and France.[20] It would be foolish to over-emphasise the outlaw element in the armies of the period but something like ten per cent of those who fought for England were conditionally pardoned outlaws, some three quarters of whom were likely to have been guilty of manslaughter or murder.[21]

After the great victory of Crécy, the capture of Calais, the successes in arms of the English in Gascony and the defeat of the Scots at Neville's Cross, any English commander could count on a fervent rush of recruits ready to seek fortune and the comradeship of arms on a full tide of national feeling. The capture of a Frenchman of importance could carry a ransom that amounted to a fortune for the soldier responsible. There was every kind of rich finery, weapons, furs, gold and silver, and wine in abundance to be had after a battle or the taking of a town.

---

[18] H. J. Hewitt, *The Organisation of War under Edward III 1338–62* (Manchester, 1966), ch. 7.

[19] *CCR 1339–41*, p. 636 etc.

[20] *CPR 1338–40; 1345–48, passim; 1354–57*, p. 478 etc; *1358–61*, pp. 5–16 etc.

[21] *Register of the Black Prince, IV, A.D. 1351–1365* (1933), pp. 237–75 etc.

The gradual changes in methods of recruitment to the English armies during the early part of the fourteenth century and the whole period under review will be familiar, but it is worth noticing some of the experiences and duties of Commissioners of Array: in 1341, for instance, they issued a writ to recruit for service 160 archers from Northampton and Rutland. In this case Rutland was charged with raising forty archers, but the county protested that Northamptonshire contained twenty-six hundreds, 'whereof the smallest is larger than the whole of Rutland', and an adjustment was made.[22] The number raised often fell short of the number projected, but the arrayers did their best to choose, test for the skills the archers should have acquired or maintained at the local butts, and array 'les meillors et plus suffisants, les plus forcibles et plus vigerous archers',[23] to clothe, equip, and where necessary mount them, to pay them, and send them with a leader to a collecting place, or hold them ready for departure. The feeble were to be avoided and the 'ailing and weakly' were sent home from the ports of embarkation, even from abroad. Men could buy out their services for 'reasonable fines', but, when the feeling for success was high, the proportion that did so was small. Exemption could be granted where there was need.

It was usual for writs to contain some mention of clothing, 'gowns', 'hoods', 'one suit' apiece and so on, which we can assume was uniform of a kind, though details of such dress are limited. Archers raised in Cheshire and Flint were to be provided with woollen 'short coats' and hats, half green and half white, green on the right, white on the left,[24] and it seems every group raised from those areas during Edward III's reign was so dressed. The uniforms were sometimes delivered at the points of array, sometimes in London.

Cheshire archers, marching to Sandwich for embarkation in 1346, were paid for the period of their journey.[25] Though not all counties treated their men so well, the Cheshire practice became gradually more widespread. In the following year recruits were given sixteen days' wages in advance for the journey from Chester to Calais, and in 1355 they had twenty-one days' wages to reach Plymouth. Obviously advance payment was essential if travelling troops were to eat properly on the journey without ruthlessly living off the land. Sometimes counties paid these travelling allowances to an agreed point, after which they were 'at the king's charges'.[26] The usual

---

22 *CCR 1341–3*, p. 190.
23 Treaty Roll, PRO C 76/22 (20 Edward III) and Hewitt, *Organisation of War*, p. 37.
24 *Register of the Black Prince*, I, pp. 13, 14, 49.
25 Cheshire County Court Rolls (Chetham Society) 1925, xliii–liv, p. 115.
26 Hewitt, *Organisation of War under Edward III*, pp. 40–1.

arrangement was for arrayed men to march to their county boundaries without pay, from there to the point of embarkation at the county's expense, and from then on to be paid by the king, even if there were delays before sailing.[27]

In 1345, the year before Crécy, while the king was collecting his army of invasion, 125 Staffordshire archers assembled at Lichfield on May 25th, and with six days' pay in their pockets (probably 18*d.*) set off for Southampton and duly arrived in a week; 100 Shropshire men met at Bridgnorth on 12 May, and set off for Sandwich with 1*s.* 9*d.* each; but twenty-two Buckinghamshire bowmen who gathered at Aylesbury on 10 May had to be content with 6*d.* each to reach Sandwich. The organisation of archers and other troops on the march was by 'hundreds' and 'vintaines' of twenty, each county contingent going in charge of a leader appointed by the king, who carried the wages and the nominal roll and was responsible for getting his charges safely to their port.[28]

At Yarmouth in 1340, 30 ships were provided by the town for forty days' service as troopers, and they were victualled at the town's expense. The bailiffs' accounts show that, apart from the foodstuffs, 60,400 gallons of ale, supplied by Johanna Hikkeson, Peter Grymbolp and John Gayter, were taken on board, at a cost to the bailiffs, hence the townsfolk, of £251 13*s.* 4*d.*[29] The allowance seems to have been one gallon a day to each of the men in the ships.

From all over Wales and England came the weapons of war — swords, knives, spears and lances from the iron-producing areas, bought and provided by the counties; arrowheads of all the different designs and weights; there were 4,000 from Chester Castle in 1359, 52*s.* 5*d.* the lot;[30] arrowheads had to be 'well brazed, and hardened at the points with steel';[31] shafts and feathers, mostly goose-wing feathers, bowstaves and made bows were constantly demanded. Later orders give an indication of earlier demands: in February 1417 six feathers from every goose in twenty southern counties were to be at the Tower by 14 March.[32] On 1 December 1418, sheriffs were ordered to supply 1,190,000 goose feathers by

27 PRO E 372/184 (Pipe Roll, 13 Edward III).
28 PRO E 372/190 (Pipe Roll, 19 Edward III), m. 6; Hewitt, *Organisation of War under Edward III*, p. 42.
29 PRO E 101/22/25; Hewitt, *Organisation of War under Edward III*, p. 52.
30 *Accounts of the Chamberlains and other Officers of the County of Chester, 1301–60*, ed. R. Stewart Brown (Record Society of Lancashire and Cheshire, 1910), p. 273.
31 *CPR 1358–61*, p. 323.
32 *Foedera*, IX, p. 436.

Michaelmas.[33] Year by year the orders went out to replace the stocks that were sent out to the archers.

Bows were divided into two kinds, 'white', which cost about 1s. 6d. each or 12 deniers, and 'painted' which were 2s. or 18d., a more expensive article.[34] No one knows what these designations meant. Yew bows come into both categories, so if 'white' were fairly raw, not long-seasoned bows, 'green' staves, which in the case of yew would show a gleaming ivory colour on the sapwood back that fades with age, that would suggest that 'painted' bows were of thoroughly seasoned staves, treated with some sort of paint or varnish, as we treat them now, to inhibit the drying out of the last vestiges of liquid in the wood, that final ten per cent or so that stops a bow becoming too brittle.

As they were collected from local manufacturers, the bows were packed in canvas and the arrow-sheaves corded together for stowage in wooden tuns.[35] These were in turn stacked in carts and wagons which were hired for the purpose, covered with tarpaulins of horse-hide, pulled by teams of two to eight horses, and accompanied by clerks who kept the tallies, saw to the delivery and got receipts in exchange. The orders sent out to counties were not always filled in one consignment. Some would come in early and the rest would be promised to follow as soon as possible; and some orders were never completely honoured. A thousand sheaves of arrows ordered from Hereford on one occasion dwindled to 363 sheaves actually delivered.[36] The orders were not regular yearly demands. In times of truce fewer orders were sent out, but whenever war was renewed massive quantities of arrows would be received at the Tower of London alone.[37] In 1356 the Chamberlain of Chester learned that 'no arrows can be obtained from England because the King has ... taken for his use all the arrows that can be found anywhere there'.[38] He then had to get for the Prince of Wales, 1,000 bows, 2,000 sheaves of arrows and 400 gross of bowstrings, requisition all available immediately and make certain that production continued until the order was fulfilled.

Available figures show that in 1359, the year of a new royal expedition after the truce, the counties supplied over 850,000 arrows to the Tower, and about 20,000 bows and 50,000 bowstrings.[39] That does not include already existing stocks, nor the fact that the orders continued to pour in to

---

[33] *CPR, 1416–22*, p. 178.
[34] PRO E 101/392/14.
[35] PRO E 372/191 m. 11.
[36] PRO E 372/201.
[37] See for example William Rothwell's accounts in PRO E 101/392/14.
[38] *Register of the Black Prince, III*, 23.
[39] *CCR 1354–60*, pp 574 and 601–2. Also PRO E 101/392/14 etc.

the suppliers for more and more of everything, nor the fact that large quantities of arms went direct to the appropriate ports. If one accepts the idea of 6,000 archers shooting off half a million arrows in one of the rare major engagements, then the production of a million arrows in a year would seem too low a figure, but it should be remembered that, from a million arrows shot off, some proportion would be recovered. Every arrow that quit the string in battle was not a lost arrow.

The cartage problem is a tricky one. A million arrows might weigh about 40 tons, and that, in the wagonage of the day, and in relation to the poor roads and rough country to be crossed, would represent a large and cumbrous part of the baggage train; but the argument of the difficulty of carriage suggesting that carriage was not achieved is a poor one. Armour had to be carried as well, tents and pavilions, food, spare bows, guns, sulphur and saltpetre, the whole equipment of the field kitchens and so forth. 40 tons of arrows, those vital components of English success in arms, may have been hard to transport, but it is quite certain that arrows were carried in great quantity.

By the time Henry VIII was campaigning against the French, taking a leaf out of Henry V's book, we can see many more details of transport. For example in 1513 his massive army of invasion marched in three 'wards' or 'battles' just as in Edward III's time, though the proportion of archers to other arms had dropped by then to one in three, or less. In one of these wards, of approximately 15,000 men, there were 90 vehicles allowed for spare weapons and equipment. 5,200 in parcels of 400 were carried in thirteen wagons; 86,000 bowstrings in twenty barrels were in two wagons; and 240,000 arrows needed twenty-six wagons, a little under 10,000 arrows a wagon.[40] Possibly in this case the artillery and its ammunition needed the big wagons, so that small carts were used for arrow-transport, and possibly in the past the bigger wagons with larger teams of oxen or horses were used for bows and arrows, which would have much increased each load and lessened the number of vehicles.

So where do such facts and figures leave us in relation to the Battle at Neville's Cross? Before looking at the role of the archers according to contemporary sources, I return to Professor Prestwich. I do so because it seems to me that again and again in his late medieval studies he understands the development of the archer arm and its tactical deployment, and in such understanding stands as a lonely eminence among most medieval historians addressing the question of the longbow's effective influence on warfare in the thirteenth, fourteenth and fifteenth centuries. In

---

[40]   C. G. Cruickshank, *Army Royal: Henry VIII's Invasion of France, 1513* (Oxford, 1969), p. 78 and London, British Library, MS Stowe 146, pp. 60–8.

his *Armies and Warfare in the Middle Ages: The English Experience*[41] he writes:

> The crucial role of archery was to deter, slow and even halt an enemy advance. Once the English developed in the fourteenth century their tactics of fighting from a defensive position, archery frequently proved devastating, and the longbow was a true battle-winning weapon. Horses were especially vulnerable to arrows, but the Scots discovered to their cost at Neville's Cross that archery was also effective against their massed defensive formations on foot, compelling them to take the fight to the English with disastrous results.

There you have the nub of the argument and the basic position of the longbow and the archer arm throughout the Hundred Years War. Add to that some of the revealed facts concerning the strength, range and penetration of the weapon and its missiles and the whole picture, though never complete, is vastly clearer than it was before.

What can we add to the detail of Neville's Cross from contemporary chronicles and letters? The answer, sadly, is not a great deal. The absurd biblical paean against the Scots by the *Lanercost Chronicle*[42] only helps us with the battle beginning 'about the third hour' with 'arrows flying', 'but few Englishmen killed', and 'nearly the whole army of Scotland either captured or slain'. It hinders us with a wholly absurd claim that King David Bruce had with him 10,000 archers. If he had even a third of that number, what on earth were they doing during the battle?

The *Anonimalle Chronicle* of St Mary's Abbey in York,[43] probably relying on the same source, but dispensing with the invective, is helpful about location: King David, it says, advanced 'from Beaurepaire (now Bearpark) ... devers la Nevyle Croice pres de Dorem ... son host en trois batailles dyvyse', and continues that the English, using the same triple division, drew up their array 'joust la croice de Nevylle avandite'.

A letter of commendation sent from His Majesty's Tower of London, three days after the battle speaks of an English victory at Durham.[44] A letter from Prior Fossor, however, provides more accurate information, and demonstrates that the battle was fought between Durham City and Bearpark.[45] That fixed point, together with the knowledge we have of the direction of approach of each army, and the lie of the land even today suggests the very probable positions of each army and the course of the battle, in broad terms, fought, as it was then, on open moorland. The Scots

---

[41] M. Prestwich, *Armies and Warfare in the Middle Ages: the English Experience* (New Haven and London 1996), p. 324.

[42] Document c.

[43] Document d.

[44] *Rot. Scot.*, I, 677.

[45] Document b.

advanced from Bearpark, the English from Bishop Auckland via Merrington.

David Smurthwaite of the National Army Museum, a battlefield scholar of distinction, in his thorough examination of the sources and location of the battle for the English Heritage Battlefield Report comes to the following conclusions (as, it must be said, does Colonel A. H. Burne in *More Battlefields of England*):[46] that Neville's Cross stands on a narrow belt of level ground about 300 feet high. To the east the ground falls away sharply some 200 feet; to the west is the River Browney, with steep banks; that the Neville's Cross ridge is approximately 1,000 yards wide at its broadest, and that on that front the English drew up their three battles.

Andrew of Wyntoun's *Orygynale Cronykil of Scotland*,[47] a Scottish source from about 1420, but possibly deriving from more contemporary accounts, speaks of

The Inglis archerys come so nere
That wyn to thame welle nere mycht thai.

It must have been at this opening stage of the battle on the Scottish right, the English left, that, galled by English archery, Sir John Graham, on the right, asked King David Bruce, in the centre, for 100 knights to ride down the archers from their flank, and that being refused, he tried with his own following and was quickly put out of action. In general the Scottish right was in trouble quite early on, it seems, partly due to 'ditches and dykes',[48] the latter possibly meaning 'walls', and both of which could have related to Beaurepaire boundaries; and partly due to the westward and southward double fall-away of ground which must have made considerable difficulties for the Scots.

The Scots right, defeated, fell inwards towards King David's central division, where it appears the toughest fighting took place. At some time during this right-wing and central-division fighting, says the Sampson letter, twice the English archers and footsoldiers were forced to give ground, before the men-at-arms could stabilise the situation 'bien tant que les archers et comunes reassemblerent'. Incidentally the same source speaks of the battle lasting from 'nones to vespers' ('l'heure de noen tantq'a l'heure de vespres'), that is from early afternoon to five or six p.m. Others interpret it as 'noon to vespers', making it a six-hour fight. What particularly intrigues me is this double fall-back of the archers and other infantry. Why did they fall back? Is it, rather, possible that after early success they twice withdrew tactically to allow the English men-at-arms to hold the ground while they

---

[46] A. H. Burne, *More Battlefields of England* (1952), pp. 115–126.

[47] Document h.

[48] *Ibid.*

either refilled their quivers, or regrouped for a flank advance on the Scottish centre, a move which happened in any case. Or did the English left-flank archers fall back to refuse the possible flanking movement of the Scottish right?

Numbers engaged are subject to the usual medieval exaggeration, and we are reduced largely to conjecture. The English Heritage report suggests 700 English men-at-arms, plus 10,000 archers, hobelars and other infantry. Burne suggests roughly Agincourt numbers for the English: short of 1,000 men-at-arms and 5,000 or 6,000 archers and others. The Scots are reckoned at some 10,000 to 15,000, though there are wild suggestions of double that number. Most responsible interpreters suggest the Scottish right was 'increasingly funnelled between the Browney to the west and the precipitous slopes bordering Crossgate Moor to the east'[49] (English Heritage Report) and that 'the ravine south of Arbour House would have reduced space still further as the Scots came within striking distance' of the English left battle. Burne thinks the English front rank at the outset was probably composed almost entirely of archers. I think that is quite likely, just as I think it is likely, and borne out by one contemporary account of Agincourt – but that takes us in to a whole argument about tactics, local command, and discipline in late medieval battle, which is not to be entered into here.

What we may argue with fair certainty is that, however hard the hand to hand fighting between men-at-arms of both armies on the English left and centre, the Battle of Neville's Cross was greatly influenced by English archery, and not greatly influenced by Scottish archery. When one fills out that vague likelihood with the simple facts of research and experiment derived from what was revealed by the *Mary Rose* archery finds, it is clear to see that in the English force there was a high number of quick-moving mounted archers (Lancashire alone contributed 960 horsed archers as against 240 foot archers) and that with their controlled, dismounted shooting from 300 yards at the outset, when with heavy arrows they could pierce mail and plate, and with increasing devastation as the range lessened, they contributed handsomely to a victory which reflected not only the appalling slaughter of the French attacks at Crécy two months earlier, but a victory of a sort that would be repeated at Agincourt, at Verneuil and other set-piece battles until the French learned not to attack massed archery in a prepared position, and to develop their gunpowder artillery to the point where it could blow military archery to the winds.

[80 *lbs* = 36.2 kg; 100 *lbs* = 45.3 kg; 150 *lbs* = 67.9 kg; 180 *lbs* = 81.5 kg; 200 yds = 182 m; 300 yds = 273 m; 400 yds = 364 m.]

---

[49]   David Smurthwaite (National Army Museum, London), report prepared for English Heritage Battlefields Panel, 1995.

Illustrative Documents

MARK ARVANIGIAN AND ANTONY LEOPOLD

(a) Letter from Prior John Fossor to Thomas Hatfield, Bishop of Durham[1]

Although we suppose that various letters have been sent by a great many people to your reverence about these deeds done by the cruel race of Scots in English lands, desiring nevertheless to increase your joy, just as we had planned, to restore your soul we bring news in these letters for your lordship to hear.

Shortly after the feast of the archangel St Michael, the aforesaid Scots, in a state of complete excitement, and with a multitude of men-at-arms and foot soldiers – who, just as we heard afterwards from several of them, did not believe that all the people of both France and England could resist them, even if their men had been greatly inflamed together – invading the country of England, they cruelly ravaged all the lands through which they passed with fire and murderous swords, with scant regard for age or sex; and among these evil deeds which they atrociously committed, they captured the fortress of Liddel, which was held by Walter de Selby, and killed whomsoever they found within it. Afterwards, however, as the Scots passed by another fortress, called *Haydenhall*,[2] near Corbridge, it was surrendered to them, to save the lives of the inhabitants.

Next, continuing for a day's journey, on a fine October day around nine, they came near to Durham City, showing themselves upon the moor of Bearpark, by arranging their battle lines, as if all ready to fight. But then, without further ado, leaving the moor, they wheeled around toward our manor of Bearpark, and spent the whole night within the park, not one of them remaining outside, just as we know with certainty. The venerable father, the Lord Archbishop of York, and the other magnates who were with him, whose names we believe you should have heard from others more fully than from us, concealed themselves upon the hill that night in your park of Auckland. Then, on the following day, namely 17 October, hearing our men moving up to the moor of Bearpark, of which I spoke previously, the Scots prepared themselves to fight with battle lines drawn

---

[1] Translated from *Historical Papers and Letters from the Northern Registers*, ed. J. Raine (RS 61; London, 1873), pp. 387–9.

[2] Aydon Castle.

up upon the same moor, next to our park. Thereafter, from about the hour of terce until nones,[3] they remained there, banners flying, between Durham City and the aforesaid manor of Bearpark, with little ground between them. At that hour, to the greater joy of the people of the English Church, both sides fought strenuously, bitterly and very fiercely. However, God Almighty, in Whose hands lay the cords of the kingdom, and, just as He pleases Himself, wounds and heals, humbles and exalts, He provided the English with a miraculous victory over the Scots, restoring to those inhabitants of the northern parts, whom the Scots long oppressed, the joy of freedom for which they had yearned.

In this conflict, David, who called himself King of the Scots, was captured, gravely wounded by an arrow in the face; indeed, many valiant men of Scotland were slain and lay strewn about over the moor of Bearpark, miserably exposed, the names and number of whom I certainly need not recount to you; in any event, you will have them related sufficiently by others. Nonetheless, many were captured, of whom one, though not valiant, is nonetheless renowned for his malice, William Douglas; his name and others are enclosed in the document presented to you. Few of us in the said battle were killed.

The place in which this battle took place, as mentioned above, is known to be sited between the City of Durham and a certain hill called Findon; a hill whose name is believed to be taken from a certain premonition, since it can truly be called Findon, as in 'bringing to an end' or 'brought to an end'.[4] For the name, as held by common opinion is interpreted as bringing to an end the pitiful discord which prevailed between English and Scots over the course of many years, by the working of His power which knows no bounds.

---

[3]   *c.* 8.30 a.m. to *c.* 2.00 p.m.

[4]   A play on 'Findon', in French 'fin don', or gives end.

(b) Thomas Sampson's Letter to his Friends[5]

My good lords, friends and companions, since you wanted good news from our region, I send you report of the Battle of Durham.

To the honour of God and our lord the King of England, know that in the year of our lord Jesus Christ 1346, and the twentieth year of the reign of our lord King Edward, may God protect him, on the eighth day of October Sir David, king of the Scots, first anointed by the authority of Pope John XXII, descendant of St Peter the apostle of Rome, after assembling the full power of Scotland, in his great pride entered the land of the English toward the region of Carlisle. With him was the Steward of Scotland and the Earls of Moray, Fife, Strathearn, Menteith, Sutherland, March, Dunbar, and Wigtown; nobles and barons included Sir William Douglas, Sir William Mowbray, Sir John Sinclair, Keith, Haliburton, Ramsay and others, whose names are included and written on the back [of this account], and others who are still unknown. There were around 2,000 bannerets, knights, and men-at-arms; about 20,000 other armed men; and nearly 40,000 soldiers with lances, axes, and bows. And they turned toward the tower of Liddel and besieged and assaulted it very fiercely. Sir Walter de Selby, keeper of the said castle, with his sons and a further forty good men, defended it most nobly, killing many Scots. But in the end, the Scots captured the castle, its guardian and all those inside, and they were put to a shameful death. Alas! They are mourned as proud knights.

And the said David was of such evil that, for the sake of his own pride, through their threats and arrogance they trespassed into the region of Carlisle and parts of Westmorland near Tynedale and Teesdale, through the county of Extildesham[6] and into the bishopric of Durham, burning, destroying, plundering, looting, and creating all of the havoc and all the dishonour that they could around the City of Durham, and they slept and lodged in the park of Bearpark[7] near Durham. There they put up their tents and pavilions of the richest and noblest sort, the likes of which had not been seen in these parts for a long time, and they provided themselves with victuals for a long time.

These things came to the notice of the honourable lord in God William, by his grace Archbishop of York primate of England, and to other great men with lands in the north, the Earl of Angus, the Lords Percy,

---

[5] Translated from *Oeuvres de Froissart*, ed. K. de Lettenhove, V (Brussels, 1868), 489–92.

[6] Hexham.

[7] or Beaurepaire.

Mowbray, Neville, Deancourt, Mauley, Leyburne, Scrope of Musgrave, the Sheriff of York, and Sir Robert Bertram, sheriff of Northumberland. They and other nobles and bannerets assembled at Richmond and moved toward the enemy, to Barnard Castle, and from there to the castle at Auckland, where they camped in the park. And on the seventeenth day of October in the aforesaid year of our lord Jesus Christ in defence of the realm of England, and of the Holy Church and its people, they moved to Durham City against the enemy. And the king of the Scots moved against them with all of his might.

And they arrayed and ordered their ranks and divisions on one side and the other. In the first line of our party were Lords Percy, Neville, Mauley, Scrope of Musgrave, the Sheriff of Northumberland, and Sir Andrew FitzRalph with the banner. In the second rank were the lord bishop, the Earl of Angus, the lord of Deancourt, Sir Roger de la Zouche and Sir Ralph Hastings, the Provost of Beverley, and the bannerets of Turville, Notre Dame, and St John. In the third rank and rearguard were the lord of Mowbray, the lord of Leyburn, and the Sheriff of York. And with us there were a good thousand men-at-arms, more than a thousand hobelars and more than 10,000 archers, and a good 20,000 foot soldiers taken solely from the region between Trent and Humber.

They assembled and fought well and for a very long time, from the hour of Nones[8] until the hour of Vespers,[9] until the enemy was fully defeated in the battle. Twice our archers and soldiers retreated, but our men-at-arms stood firm and fought stubbornly until the archers and foot soldiers reassembled. And God, by his grace and virtue, gave us victory. And so King David and the Scots were defeated in the battle and were killed and captured. King David was taken prisoner by John de Coupland, and the Earl of Moray and other earls, nobles and barons of the Scottish peerage were captured and killed. Their names are included and listed more fully on the back.

The lord of Lucy, who came hurrying to the battle as fast as he could with a great number of men-at-arms and was not there on the day, encountered the fleeing enemy and pursued them relentlessly, and many of them were slain and captured, until they were able to reach the Scottish Marches.

The lord of Tiptoft, custodian of the town of Berwick, wisely remained in the town with his men until he had heard news of the defeat, and then he went out in force to meet the enemy and set to capturing and slaying them, up to the castle of Dunbar, so that only a valiant few escaped, God's grace being upon them.

8   *c.* 1.30 to 2.00 p.m.
9   *c.* 5.00 p.m.

The names of the Scottish lords who died in the Battle of Durham on 17 October, which can be known are: the Earl of Moray, the Earl of Stratheam, the Steward of Scotland, the Earl Patrick, Sir John Haliburton, Sir Henry Ramsay, Sir Thomas Boyd, Sir John Stewart, Sir David Hay, Sir Edward Keith and his brother, Sir John Crawford, Sir John Lindsay, Sir Phillip Meldrum, Sir Henry Ramsay, Sir Alexander More, Sir Humphrey Kirkpatrick and his brother, Sir Alexander Strachan the father, Sir Alexander the son, Sir Ness Ramsay, Sir Adam Nixon, Sir Gilbert Inchmartin, Sir Payton Hering, Sir John Strachan, Sir Robert Maitland and his brother, Sir Maurice Murray, and around 540 other knights and men-at-arms who were killed in battle, excepting those who were killed in the chase and the foragers, estimated at 12,000 and more.

The names of those captured in the battle: Sir David Bruce, by John de Coupland, the Earl of Menteith by John de Latoun and T. of York; the Earl of Fife by Robert Ogle, the Earl of Wigtown, Sir Malcolm Fleming; and Sir William Douglas by Sir Robert Bertram; Sir William Livingstone by Sir William de la Zouche; Sir William Mowbray, Sir John Sinclair, Sir David fitz Robert fitz Walter,[10] Sir John Stewart, Sir Roger Kirkpatrick, Sir John Steward the brother, Sir David Annand, Sir William Ramsay, Sir James de Lorraine, Sir William Douglas the brother, Sir David Annand, Sir William Ramsay the son, Sir Adam Moigne, Sir Walter Haliburton, Sir Henry Douglas the brother of Sir William, Sir John Douglas, Sir John Hume, Sir William More, Sir John Sandilands, Sir Henry Ker, Sir Patrick captured by Sir Ralph Neville. And a great number of other knights and squires were captured, many of whose names are still uncertain.

The names of the English barons who were slain in the said battle: Sir Rohaut Richmond, Sir John Rothsay, Sir William Crathorne, Robert Lannington, William Crepping, William Child, Michael Huddleston, John Dyuelyn, clerk.

The names of the English who were knighted on that day: Sir Piers Bavent, Sir Marmaduke Constable, Sir Ralph Hastings the son, Sir Thomas Malesors, Sir Henry Nottingham, Sir John Monces, Sir Piers Nuttile. In the company of the lord bishop: Sir John Mauleuerer the father, Sir John his son, Sir Roger Trumpington, Sir Roger Hewick. In the company of Lord Mowbray: Sir William Heron, Sir John his brother, Sir Piers Mauley, Sir Thomas Bentley, Sir Thomas Middleton, Sir Thomas Ask. In the company of Lord Percy: Lord Neville, Sir Simon Ward, Sir Henry Vavasour, Sir Thomas Metham the son. In the company of Lord Neville: Sir Robert Hansard, Sir Nicholas Turney, Sir William Crathorne. Killed on the day: Sir Acres Halnathby, Sir Robert Fritheby. In the company of Sir Thomas Rokeby: Sir Matthew Redman, Sir Gilbert Broomshead of Kendall.

---

[10]   Correctly, David fitz Walter fitz Gilbert.

The array of battle for the Scots. In the front row the Steward of Scotland, the Earl of Fife, the Earl of Strathearn, and the Earl of Wigtown. In the middle guard, Sir David Bruce, Sir William Douglas, and the Earl Patrick. In the rear were the Earl of Moray and other bannerets. And men-at-arms they brought to England numbered about 2,000, with 20,000 other armed men, and 40,000 other common soldiers. And absolutely all of those came to the battle excepting those who were killed at the pele of Liddel.

(c) Chronicle of Lanercost[11]

At dawn the next morning, that is, on the eve of St Luke the Evangelist, William Douglas left the Scottish camp with 500 men to ravage and plunder the country. Therefore, the Scots took their spoil in the morning, but in the evening, the English divided the plunder. For on that morning, while the Scots were ravaging the town of Merrington, bad weather and thick fog suddenly descended upon them. Hearing the noise of horses and the sound of armed men, there fell on them such terrible dread that William and those with him were unsure which way to turn. Then, to their surprise, and just as God had willed it, they stumbled unexpectedly upon the army of the lord Archbishop of York and Thomas Rokeby, at whose hands many were killed. However, William escaped for the moment, with 200 armed men mounted on horses, though not without wounds. Then, Robert Ogle, a man of great strength, and not lacking skill in the art of war, pursued them over the plains and hills, killing many by his own hand, and he did not rest until, by a large pool in a wooded valley, his warhorse, completely exhausted by the chase, could go no further.

William then returned to the Scottish army, hot and shouting very vigorously, 'David! rise quickly; look, all the English are attacking us.' David replied that this was not possible, saying, 'There are none in England but wretched monks, disreputable priests, swineherds, cobblers and skinners; they dare not face me, I am safe enough;' but they did face him, and as was clear afterwards, they were only gently testing him. 'Certainly,' said William, 'O feared king, saving your peace you will find otherwise. There are many valiant men coming swiftly upon us, and they want to fight.' Just before he said these words, two black monks came from Durham to treat with David for a truce. 'Behold,' said David, 'these false monks speak with me craftily, for they detain us here in conference so that the English army might attack us suddenly while we are thus deceived.' Therefore, he ordered them to be taken and beheaded at once, but by then, all of the Scots were so busy that the monks secretly escaped, joyful and unharmed, walking back home without any loss. David, like another Nebuchadnezzar, pompously enlarged the fringes of his standard, ritually and repeatedly affirming himself King of the Scots without any obstruction. He ordered his breakfast be prepared, and said he would return to it when he had run through the English with the point of his sword. But, soon after, so very soon after, all of his servants were in such hurry that they let the food drop into the fire. Hence, David, with great foolishness, sought to

---

[11]   Translated from *Lanercost*, pp. 348–51.

catch fish with a net, and therefore lost many, and caught few. And so he failed to complete the agreement he had concluded, because, like Aman and Achitopel, what he had planned for us befell him instead.

Thus, trusting in his people, David called the Scots together – men keen for war, yet about to be scattered in defeat – and, like another Jabin against Joshua, assembled three great and strong columns to attack the English. He stationed Earl Patrick in the first rank, but he, like a prattling fool, requested the third, declining to lead the first line, more from cowardice than keenness. The Earl of Moray at once took his place, and so became chief of the first division, and later perished in the conflict. With him were many brave men of Scotland, such as the Earl of Strathearn, the Earl of Fife, John Douglas, brother of William Douglas, Alexander Ramsay, and many other valiant earls, barons, knights and squires, raging together with unrestrained fury against the English, surging forward, unwilling to stop, confident in their own strength, as like Satan, swelling with enormous pride, they sought to reach the stars. King David himself led the second rank, not, however, the David who put ten thousand men to flight in battle whom they sang about in the choir, but the David of whom they proclaimed aloud that his stench and excrement defiled the altar. He brought with him the Earl of Buchan, Malcolm Fleming, Alexander Strachan, father and son without the holy spirit, the Earl of Menteith, and many others whom we do not know, and if we did, it would be tedious to relate them all. In the third line was Earl Patrick, who would be better called 'earl absent' in his homeland, for he came late, but did very well, always standing far off, like another Peter, and not wishing to see the end of the affair. In this conflict he harmed no one, because he intended to take holy orders, to celebrate mass for the Scottish dead, knowing the worth of prayer to the Lord for the repose of the departed; indeed he was a priest at that very time, because he led the others to flight himself. His associate was Robert Stewart, and if one was worthless, the other was nothing. Overwhelmed by cowardice, he broke his promise to God that he would never wait for the first blow in battle, and he fled with the priest, like one good cleric assisting at the mass of the other. Turning their backs, these two fled valiantly with their force and entered Scotland unscathed, and so they led the dance, leaving David to dance to his own tune.

About the hour of terce, the English fell on the Scots not far from Durham, with the Earl of Angus in the front line, a noble man among all the English, of great boldness and wonderful righteousness, always ready to fight spiritedly for his country, whose great deeds no tongue could tell. Lord Henry Percy – like another Judas Maccabeus, son of Matthias – was another fierce warrior, small but wise, encouraging all to stand together on the field of battle by charging forth into the enemy's front line. Lord Ralph

Neville, a true and powerful man, bold, astute and greatly to be feared, fought so fiercely in the said battle that, as borne out afterward, the marks of his blows remained with the enemy. Nor was Lord Henry Scrope last, but instead held his station in the forefront of the battle, pushing down the foe. The Archbishop of York, leader of the second rank, called his men together, and blessed them all, which, by the grace of God, had a good effect.

There was also another bishop of the order of Friars Minor, who, for his blessing, ordered the English to fight strongly, always adding that, under the heaviest penalty, none should spare the Scots; and when he fell on the enemy he gave them no indulgence from punishment or sin, but great penance and good absolution with a certain club; he had such power at the time that he absolved the Scots from all lawful acts without any confession with the said club.

In the third line, John Mowbray, who made his name in the affair, was full of grace and goodness, and his good fortune and renown has spread far and wide through great and deserved praise, for he and all his men acted so well that they will have honour for a very long time. Lord Thomas Rokeby, just like a noble leader, set before the Scots such a drink that, after they had tried it once, they had no desire for another taste; and thus he was an example to all onlookers of how to fight bravely for the sacred cause of the homeland. John de Coupland delivered such blows among the foe that it is said that those who felt his hefty clouts were able to fight no longer. Then, with trumpets sounding, shields clashing, arrows flying, spears piercing, wounded men shrieking, and troops crying out, arms shattered, heads split open, and, O woe! many prone on the field, the conflict ended at about the hour of Vespers, with the Scots fleeing and our men slaying them. Praise and honour to the Most High! On that day, the English had the victory. And so by the prayers of the blessed Virgin Mary and Saint Cuthbert, confessor of Christ, David and the flower of Scotland fell, by the justice of God, into a pit which they had dug themselves.

Thus a battle was fought between English and Scots, as mentioned, in which few English were killed, but nearly the whole of the Scottish army were captured or killed; for in that battle were slain Robert, earl of Moray[12] and Maurice, earl of Strathearn, along with the pick of the army of Scotland; moreover, David, so-called King of Scotland, with the Earls of Fife, Menteith, and Wigtown, and William Douglas, and with many men-at-arms, were captured. Soon thereafter, the said David, king of the Scots, was brought to London with many of the nobler captives, and thrown into gaol, where the Earl of Menteith was drawn, hung and

---

[12]   He was not in fact Robert, but John.

quartered, and his limbs were sent to various places in England and Scotland. However, one of the said captives, to wit Malcolm Fleming, earl of Wigtown, was not brought to London with the other on account of his infirmity, but O woe! escaped at Bothal, through the treachery of his guard, said to be Robert de la Vale, and hence returned to Scotland without paying a ransom.

After the aforementioned Battle of Durham, the lord of Angus and Ralph Neville went to Scotland – Henry Percy being sick – and received the castle of Roxburgh under certain conditions, ranged through the marches of Scotland, imposing tribute on certain men from beyond the Scottish Sea, and received oaths of fealty from others, and returned to England, though not without some damage to their army.

(d) The Anonimalle Chronicle[13]

In this same year, 1346, on the sixth day of October, which is the day of the virgin St Faye, David Bruce, king of the Scots, with all his earls, barons, knights and squires, that is to say the Counts of Moray, Fife, Menteith, Carrick, Sutherland, Strathearn, Lennox, Wigtown, Angus, Mar, Ross, Earl Patrick, the Steward of the Scots, Ranald the Small, leader of the people of the Outer Isles, William Douglas, Alexander Strachan the father and Alexander the son and several other noble and valiant men. The number of men at arms was 1,500; and there were more than 40,000 hobelars, archers and earls. The King of the Scots entered England with all his host without title or right and they made their way together to the fortress of Liddel and vigorously assaulted it day and night. Sir Walter of Selby, a hardy and valiant knight, guardian of the said pele, strongly defended it with his men and wounded several of the Scots and killed some. But on the fifth day, the Scots filled the ditches of the pele with trees and branches and knocked down the walls. Hence they rushed in on the English and captured the pele by force, and they killed all those whom they found inside, except for one who secretly escaped.[14]

Then the said Sir Walter of Selby, guardian of the said fortress, seeing that there was no way to escape approached the King of the Scots imploring and asking from him that he might have combat with one of his men in the field as befitted a knight, and thus end his life and not be killed as a robber or murderer. But David, angry and ungracious, did not want to assent to this petition, so he ordered the knight to be beheaded. Then the said Walter knelt and said, 'O noble king, since you have seen me and spoken with me and I sued in your presence, show me a drop of regal grace, because it is fitting for a king of rightful blood.' But the said David did not wish to hear this prayer, so he ordered the execution of the knight. And thus he was decapitated without confession. Soon after, God took great vengeance on the said king and his men, for they had such great joy and elation at doing evil and bringing ruin on righteous men. Then, the said king and the Scots came to the Priory of Lanercost and there they knocked down the houses and the places of sanctuary, loaded up the ornaments of the holy church and carried off all their jewels. Afterwards, they marched by Naworth Castle and the town of Redpath, destroying and devastating.

---

[13] Translated from *The Anonimalle Chronicle*, ed. V. H. Galbraith (Manchester, 1927), pp. 23–8. The close connection of this portion of the chronicle with the *Lanercost Chronicle*'s account of the battle is discussed *ibid*, pp. xxvi–xxviii.

[14] The following section is closely based on *Lanercost*.

At this time the people of the County of Carlisle, throughout Cumberland and Westmorland and Allerdale and Coupland, made a truce with the Scots for 300 marks, so that, in the bounds of Carlisle and the aforementioned lands, the Scots did not burn or devastate towns nor castles nor hamlets, and they did no harm or damage.

Then the Scots went to the Priory of Hexham and they stayed there for three days and inflicted much harm and destruction to their goods and castles. And at this time the said King of the Scots forbade the burning of four towns, Hexham, Corbridge, Darlington and Durham, for the reason that he planned to stay in these same towns in the coming winter. Then the King of the Scots and his people came from Hexham to the town of Ebchester destroying and robbing all the surrounding countryside. Afterwards, to our pleasure and their confusion David, king of the Scots, marched with his host to the wood of Bearpark, the wood of the Prior of Durham, ordering his servants and tormentors to take all the beasts, burn the towns and houses, and kill men and women in the lands around.[15]

At this same time William de la Zouche, then archbishop of York, came to Richmond to meet the Scots with a small number of men at arms, monks, canons, priests and clerks. They stayed there for one night to refresh themselves. At this time Thomas d'Umfraville, earl of Angus, Lord Deancourt, Lord Mowbray, Lord Percy, Lord Neville, Sir Henry Scrope, Sir Thomas Rokeby then sheriff of York, with their men assembled in diverse parts of the country, awaiting the arrival of the said bishop. On the fifteenth day of October the archbishop left Richmond with his retinue and came towards Barnard Castle. The next day the archbishop and the lords with their men at arms and hobelars and archers assembled in an open field and there counted their number: the men at arms numbered 800 and the hobelars and archers and common soldiers 10,000. Then they marched towards Bishop Auckland to meet the enemy together, and they pitched their tents in a pleasant wood near the town, and rested there all night at their ease. The next morning, on the eve of St Luke the Evangelist the English confessed themselves, knelt and devotedly prayed for God's aid, and took Holy Communion.[16]

That same morning, William Douglas left with 500 men from the Scottish host to destroy the land, and to forage and gather spoil. They suddenly descended on the town of Merrington. Then by a great rock the weather descended on them so heavily that neither William Douglas nor any of his company knew which was the way to return to their host, but since God so willed it, they came upon the men of the archbishop and Thomas Rokeby, who quickly attacked and defeated them, and killed a

---

[15] The following section is independent of *Lanercost*.
[16] The following section is again closely based on *Lanercost*.

great number. But William Douglas with a few of his men who were mounted on horses, survived and escaped to the great irritation of the English. Robert Ogle, squire of the north country, valiant and hardy, pursued the Scots strongly through hills and dales and killed several of them with his own hand and followed them remorselessly until his warhorse failed him after so much work by a deep pool. Then William Douglas rode towards the Scottish host, fairly hot and alarmed, and coming to the king's tent he cried with great noise and hideous clamour, like a man enraged, 'O David, David, get up quickly because the English are coming on us in battle array.' Then David got up from his bed irritated and said angrily, 'O man, that cannot be, because in England there are no men left but monks and canons, brothers and priests, swineherds and shepherds, cobblers and skinners; but all the knights are with their king overseas. And be sure that they dare not look me in the face, nor meet me on the field of battle.' Then William Douglas said, 'O noble king, save your grace, you will find otherwise, because they are valiant and vigorous men and they wish to fight you this day.' And at this news the king was joyous and happy.

At the same time these words were spoken, two monks of Durham came to treat with King David for their manors and goods. Then King David angrily said, 'See these false monks, who cleverly detain me in discussions with their devious words, so that our enemies suddenly come upon us with their forces.' So he ordered them to be taken and then to be decapitated. But at the time all the Scots were so preoccupied with their arms that they did not take note of the king's order for the execution. Hence the monks returned safely and unharmed to their house very easily. At the same time King David in pride and anger mounted his warhorse; and he dedicated his army with the seven deadly sins and ordered his servants to prepare his breakfast, and when he had killed the English, he would return to it without delay. But the servants were in such haste to flee that they left the dishes and the meats to fall into the fire and perish.[17]

Then David rode from Bearpark, where the army was camped, towards Neville's Cross, near Durham, and there the army split into three divisions. In the first Scottish rank were the Earl of Moray, the Earl of Strathearn, the Earl of Fife, Sir John Douglas brother of William Douglas, Sir Alexander Ramsay, Sir John Crawford and many other valiant men, barons, knights and squires. In the second rank – King David, the Earl of Wigtown, the Earl of Menteith, Sir Walter Haliburton, Sir Alexander Strachan the father and Sir Alexander the son and several others. In the third rank – Earl Patrick, Sir Robert Stewart, steward of the Scots, and other knights and squires and a great number of foot soldiers. Then the English knelt and devotedly prayed God for aid when they were seen by

[17] The following section is independent of *Lanercost*.

the enemy and they turned towards them in good spirits. Their men divided into three ranks, as the Scots had done. In the first English line were Thomas d'Umfraville, earl of Angus, Lord Percy, Sir Ralph Neville and Sir John Neville his son who was at the Battle of Crécy eight weeks earlier, and Sir Henry Scrope, Thomas Musgrave, Thomas Rokeby the cousin and John Huddleston, the last three being made knights that day. In the second line – Lord Mowbray, Sir Thomas Rokeby, sheriff of York, Sir William Percy, Sir Robert of Richmond, Sir Hugh Morisby, and others with them. In the third line – William de la Zouche, archbishop of York, Lord Deancourt, Ralph Hastings, Robert Ogle and John de Coupland and monks and canons and priests and clerks. Then around the hour of tierce the archbishop addressed all the English and ordered them to fight vigorously and counter the great malice of the Scots and defend their country.

Soon after, the aforementioned ranks assembled near Durham, at Neville's Cross, and fought strongly and relentlessly for a long time and two or three times rested by agreement and then fought again. In this conflict lances were shattered, swords broken, armour pierced, helms and bascinets knocked off and shields broken into pieces. But by divine grace and by the intercession of the Virgin Mary and the good confessor St Cuthbert, the Scots were defeated around the hour of vespers and many were captured and many killed. As God had willed, they left the field and the victory to the English. Robert Stewart, steward of the Scots, Earl Patrick and many of the rearguard took to flight without giving or receiving a blow from sword or lance. But the English heard of their flight and quickly gave chase. In this pursuit a great number of the Scots were captured and killed. So the English returned to their host praising God for their great victory. The following Scots were killed in this battle – the Earl of Moray, the Earl of Strathearn, Sir William Ramsay, Sir John Crawford, Sir Thomas Boyd, Sir John Stewart, Sir Alan Stewart, Sir John Stewart the brother, Sir David Hay, Sir Edward Keith and his brother, Sir William More, Sir John Lindsay, Sir Henry Ramsay, Sir Alexander More, Sir Humphrey Boyce, Sir Alexander Strachan the father and Sir Alexander the son, the most valiant knights of the land of Scotland, Sir Patrick Herring, Sir Alexander Rait, Sir William Wiseman and Sir Patrick Dunbar and a great number of common soldiers. Those captured in the battle were – the king of the Scots, David Bruce, the Earl of Menteith, the Earl of Wigtown, Sir William Douglas, Sir Henry Douglas, Sir Walter Haliburton, the Earl of Fife, Sir David Annand, Sir John Sinclair, Sir William Vaus, Sir Thomas Charteris, Sir William Livingstone, Sir William Mowbray, Sir Adam Nicholson, Sir William Cunningham and many other knights and squires; and a great number of common soldiers.[18]

---

[18]   The next paragraph is closely based on *Lanercost*.

And the said King of the Scots, with the aforementioned earls and knights were taken to London, and there, the Earl of Menteith was drawn, hung and quartered, and the quarters were sent to various cities in England. But the Earl of Wigtown, Malcolm Fleming by name, was not brought to London with the others, because by a false traitor named Robert de la Vale for a great payment and ransom he was delayed in Scotland near Bothall. After the said battle, the Earl of Angus, Sir Henry Percy, and Sir Ralph Neville entered Scotland with their forces, and the castle of Roxburgh and several others were delivered to them with certain conditions, and several Scots swore fealty to them; and then they returned to England.[19]

At this same time news came to the King of England who was at the siege of Calais of the aforementioned Battle of Durham, at which he was very joyous and often gave thanks to God for the great victory with great devotion.

---

[19]   The next paragraph is independent of *Lancercost*.

(e) The Chronicle of Meaux Abbey, Yorkshire[20]

Meanwhile David Bruce, called king of Scots, who had fled to France from the face of Edward Balliol, former king of Scotland, now returned to Scotland as an ally of the King of France. Knowing that Edward, king of England, was occupied with the siege of Calais, and that some of the magnates were journeying with the king, and to Gascony and Brittany, he gathered an army of 40,000 men, and made a vow, promising that he would either bring Edward, king of England, back from the said siege, or make the Humber the boundary of his kingdom. On 7 October he invaded England, took the castle of Liddel near Carlisle, and ordered all found in it to be beheaded. Then he led his army toward Hexham, ravaging and burning the land, sparing neither the young nor the women, killing all who were taken. William de la Zouche, archbishop of York, with his clergy, the Earl of Angus, the Lords Percy, Mowbray, Neville, Deincourt, the Baron of Bothal, and Thomas de Rokeby, sheriff of Yorkshire, collected together men and military equipment, totalling 900 men-at-arms and 9,000 archers, and set out for Auckland Park near Durham. There the people gathered, on the moor between Durham and Bearpark, around the hour of Prime,[21] Scots and English, on 17 October. Several of the Scots who were ravaging the countryside had already been killed by the English that morning. The Bishop of Durham was staying in the south in a manor he owned.[22] Both the armies, the English and the Scots, divided their men into three lines, with the archers placed on the flanks. The Scots positioned themselves in a fairly steep place to await the English. The English likewise chose a high place, about a quarter of a mile away, which they ascended, and waited for the enemy attack. But 500 English archers ran on in advance, and with their missiles forced the Scots to abandon the place they had occupied, and provoked them to seek battle. And at once all the lines of footsoldiers engaged. And the English were at first forced to withdraw somewhat; but recovering their strength repaid the Scots for their attack. At last, because of their exhaustion and the length of the fight, they rested from the fight for a time, leaning on their spears and weapons. Then, recovering their strength and their breath, they began to fight again savagely. But at last many of the Scots fell. The earl of Dunbar, Patrick, and the Steward of

---

[20] Translated from *Chronica monasterii de Melsa a fundatione usque ad annum 1396*, ed. E. A. Bond (RS 43; 3 vols., London, 1866–8), III, 60–2.

[21] Daybreak.

[22] Thomas Hatfield, bishop of Durham, had been present on Edward III's French campaign, and had fought at the battle of Crécy.

Scotland, thinking that their men were losing and the English winning, fled straightaway. Others followed. Footsoldiers, mounted on their lords' horses, sought their homeland. But David Bruce, king of Scots, was wounded in the face by an arrow, turned aside from the battle, and was captured in flight. Three earls were taken, those of Fife, Menteith and Wigtown, along with William Douglas, William Mowbray and about 100 bannerets and knights, and about 2,000 other people. The Earl of Menteith, later convicted of treason, was drawn and beheaded in London. Malcolm Fleming, earl of Wigtown, escaped from the custody of the Baron of Bothal through the treachery of an archer. And there was killed in the battle the Earl of Moray, the Earl of Stratheam, and about 2,000 chosen bannerets, knights and squires, and the rest of the people.

The events of the battle had been revealed to someone in a vision. When he was in the monastery of St Cuthbert, he saw the saint standing before him, in the place where he rests. Cuthbert rose, and went to the vestiary. There, putting on vestments, and accepting the pastoral staff in his hand, he made his way to the doors of the church, and then walked to the moor of Bearpark. The man himself followed the prelate from some distance, to find out the reason for his journey. Going round a particular place, the holy confessor blessed it, and said, 'The Lord gave me this place, and the enemy fighting there has already given me victory.' At once he returned, went to the vestiary, took off his vestments and put down the staff; and put himself back in the place from which he had arisen. King David, on the night preceding the battle, was troubled by several visions of the way the business would turn out.

(f) The Chronicle of Geoffrey le Baker[23]

While Edward, by the grace of God King of England and conqueror of France, was besieging the impregnable town of Calais, the tyrant of the French sent a great number of Genoese and other mercenaries to David, king of the Scots, with letters strongly urging him to ravage England – its fighting men having been, as noted, evacuated – and to storm castles and fortifications and take them for himself, so that the two countries could simultaneously subjugate the English with ease. Hence, around the feast of St Dionysius, David, king of the Scots, with all the power of Scotland as well as the mercenaries sent to him, invaded England, bypassing Berwick, which was defended by the English. However, after traversing the forest of Alnwick and pillaging the surrounding land, they attacked a certain manor of the Lord of Wark, called Liddel. This was defended against them for some time by Sir Walter of Selby, a most worthy knight, who at last, compelled by the numbers of the Scots, handed himself over to the victor, who took him graciously, to be held for ransom according to the custom used in French and Scottish wars. His capture was swiftly brought to the attention of David, and, though desiring pity and ransom, he ordered him to be killed. Walter entreated that he be brought alive to David's presence, and, having obtained his first wish, knelt in David's court and sought his life for ransom; but once more he was condemned to death. The knight complained of the cruelty of the tyrant's order, saying that by the ancient royal law of mercy of the kingdoms of Scotland, England and France, each petitioner might enjoy the privilege of immunity, so long as he stood in the king's sight, and that a supplicant was never refused after seeking mercy in the presence of the king. But with hard-hearted malice of a tyrant, twisting the evil rope by which the prisoner had been dragged there, and not recalling that he was ever anointed with holy oil – signifying mercy – the king ordered the two sons of the wretched knight to be strangled in front of him, as if he had been brought up on the milk of lions, and afterwards, almost mad from grief, the knight was beheaded. With God as my witness, I have enquired of many, but have never heard that this knight ever perpetrated any treachery against the King of the Scots, or any Scot; and it is his cruel and unjust killing which I believe to have been the main cause of the trials of the king and the great Scottish army, related below. Setting off from there, the wretches did not fear St Cuthbert, whom previous kings of Scotland had held in great veneration, and had enriched his monastery

---

[23]   Translated from *Chronicon Galfridi le Baker de Swynebroke*, ed. E.M. Thompson (Oxford, 1889).

with great alms, and it is said they did not hesitate to ravage his lands. Certainly they came within two miles of Durham, pillaging many of his farms, and there detained certain monks of Saint Cuthbert as captives for ransom, making a pact with the remainder for money and corn to spare their manors from further destruction.

Lamentation arose from the English of the marches fleeing in the face of the army; so Lord William de la Zouche, archbishop of York, who at the time held the king's place in that march, having called together the Bishop of Carlisle, the Earl of Angus, Lord Mowbray, Lord Percy, Lord Neville and other northern nobles with their forces, together with the archers of the county of Lancaster, went to meet the army of the Scots at the place called Neville's Cross, on the vigil of St Luke the Evangelist. The Scots did not flee, and with heads bent and covered in iron, densely drawn against the English attack, with helmets polished and shields fastened precisely, they withstood the arrows of the English at the beginning of the battle; but the first line of armed men were greeted with fatal blows. The warriors on each side stood more prepared for death than flight. You could see the Scots wearied from exertion, so terrified by the blows of axe-heads, yet standing, so that where perhaps there stood ten, each supporting the others, the felling of one with one blow meant the felling of all together; just as those who saw them slaughtered fell back. The marshall of the Scots, Earl Patrick, who had been given charge of the rearguard, when he first saw the English resist and slaughter his men, fled with all those who were prompted by his cowardice to do likewise, which the Lord Percy had prophesied that day, saying: 'The cowardice of that traitor, who never dared to resist us in the field, profits our army more than the felling of a thousand Scots.' After he had fled, the remainder, staying faithfully with their king, preferred a glorious death to an ignominious flight. Indeed, they stood together like a round tower, protecting the king in the middle, until there were barely forty left surviving, of whom not one could flee away. Finally their king, David, was captured by John de Coupland, and the rest of those who remained with the king were killed or taken for ransom, while the other fugitives were pursued as far as Prudhoe and Corbridge, and were also killed or taken for ransom.

Captured in this struggle were David Bruce, king of the Scots, the Earl of Menteith, the Earl of Fife, Lord Malcolm Fleming, the Earl of Wigtown, William Douglas, William Livingstone, Walter Haliburton, John Douglas, David Annand, John Sinclair, William Mowbray, David fitz Robert fitz Kenneth,[24] William Ramsay, Adam Moigne, John Stewart, Roger Kirkpatrick, John Hume and William More, knights; James

---

[24] Correctly, he was David fitz Walter fitz Gilbert, the head of the Hamilton family. See *Rot. Scot.*, I, 678.

Sandilands, James Lorraine, and Henry Ker, squires. Killed in the same battle were the Earl of Moray and the Earl of Strathearn; also Alexander Strachan, John Haliburton, Henry Ramsay, Ness Ramsay, Adam Nicholson, Thomas Boyd, John Stewart, Alan Stewart, David Hay, Edward Keith, John Crawford, John Kynnesey, Philip Meldrum, Henry Ramsay, Alexander More, Humphrey Boyce, Gilbert Inchmartin, Robert Maitland and his brother Humphrey Kirkpatrick, John Strachan, and Patrick Hering, knights. Besides these, many of those who fled were killed in the pursuit thereafter; but not more than those were first reported to have been dressed in the field, so the precise number of men dressed for battle and the names of those killed can be made known.

(g) The Scotichronicon, by Walter Bower[25]

The disposition for the battle; and the appearance of St Cuthbert to King David

Since for all these reasons[26] the said King David wished to take revenge on the English, he abandoned the advice of the said Sir William de Douglas, and the counsel of others prevailed. And as they hurried to the monastery of Hexham breathing threats against the English, the warriors were counted there, and the total came to only about 2,000 well-armed men, although the count included a great army of those that were lightly armed. Advancing therefore, King David and his army were encamped at Ryton, and St Cuthbert appeared to him in his sleep, bringing the mild request that the Scots should not invade or damage his lands. But the king, after discussion with the leading men of his council concerning the revelation divinely shown to him, pressed ahead, just as a snake foolishly closes his ears in response to a charmer, because they believed that the Kingdom of England was weakened in fighting-strength, devoid of men and destitute of all help. They did not believe that the men in either kingdom (that is in France or England) could resist this multitude of armed men and foot-soldiers, even if they were brought back into one force and combined their strengths together. When therefore the King of Scotland had invaded the northern parts of England in hostile fashion, and he laid waste for a fortnight with fatal fire and sword all the parts he had passed through, at length the Scots came to the land of the Church of Durham. There, spinning out what was left of their rations, and acting with the irresponsibility which they had adopted and initiated in England, on 16 October about 3 p.m. they arrived near Durham at the moor of Bearpark, showing themselves arrayed in battle-lines, with banners unfurled, ready (as it seemed) to fight if any opposed them. But at once without any further respite for refreshment they turned towards the said manor of Bearpark so that they could sleep the

---

25 *Scotichronicon by Walter Bower, in Latin and English*, ed. D. E. R. Watt *et al.* (Aberdeen and Edinburgh, 1987–), VII, 255, 257, 259, and 261. For full annotation, see this edition. We are most grateful to Professor Watt and the University of St Andrews for allowing us to reproduce this text. Although the *Scotichronicon* was written in the 1440s, the author was drawing heavily on a lost Latin chronicle of the 1390s, a work also used as a source by Andrew Wyntoun in his vernacular verse chronicle (Document h).

26 The chronicler has previously explained the French appeal to the Scots for assistance, and the Earl of Douglas's advice that King David should return to Scotland after the capture of Liddle.

more safely for the whole of that night out of danger's way in the park, with none of them remaining outside.

Meanwhile the Archbishop of York, Henry de Percy, John de Mowbray, Ralph de Neville and the Lords of Ferrers, Rokeby and Lucy, Coupland and Ogle and very many other churchmen with armed men and foot-soldiers, who had been assembled for the purpose in the Park of Auckland (which lies six miles away from the said park at Bearpark), were secretly stationing themselves during the night. The archbishop indeed and his men decided at daybreak to join battle with the Scots, though they had not thought of this beforehand. So in the end they left the park[27] and on seeing a hill near Merrington which they reckoned suitable for this clash, they climbed it to see whether the Scots were to be expected there to do business. But in the course of this, while the leaders carrying standards and the others who were with them were advancing bit by bit, the Scots followed as if not knowing what they were doing, so that before they realised where they were, they were a long way away from the place where the business had begun, and thus they moved by slow stages to Sunderland Bridge. Judging that another hill near these bridges was suitable for them to join battle, the leaders gathered there to discuss among themselves whether they should remain there to await the Scots. As they were beginning to discuss this matter, that same thing which had happened to them in the other place happened to them again. Hence as the Scots were meanwhile preparing themselves for battle, the English approached the manor of Bearpark which lay just two miles from where they were then, and took up their position on the same moor at a certain place near Durham beside the cross which is called Neville's Cross just a short distance from the said Scots. They took up their stations for the fight by dividing their men into three sections.

The battle

In the meantime while the English were positioning themselves for a battle, the King of Scotland remained still in the park with his men, unaware of the English approach. In the morning he sent Sir William de Douglas to ravage the land of the Church of Durham, and to collect booty to refresh his army. When he came upon the enemy unexpectedly, they met in a way that was sudden for both sides at a place which is called Ferryhill. But because the said Sir William de Douglas did not have the backing of a force adequate for confronting so large a multitude of adversaries, he began a

---

[27] This section, from 'So in the end they left the park...' has been modified from the translation given in Scott and Watt's edition. The Latin phraseology is somewhat obscure.

withdrawal towards the king with his men, during which he lost five hundred sturdy Scottish troops at the place called Sunderland Bridge; but Douglas himself was fortunate to escape their hands. On hearing this the Scots were thrown into confusion to an extraordinary degree. They were divided into three sections with the king in command of one, the Earl of Moray and Sir William de Douglas in command of the second, and the Earl of Dunbar and the Steward of Scotland in command of the third. But as the formations approached the line of battle, Sir John Graham requested a hundred mounted lancers to break up the English archers, so that by this means the king might more easily attack the enemy; but to tell the truth, he could not obtain even one (for no one dared to commit himself to such a risk). On this account Graham became angry and rode alone among the archers shaking his lance; he fiercely scattered them in turn, when his noble horse was killed by a flying arrow, and he only just escaped to the king scarcely with his life. At length everyone was in position and the sound of trumpets was heard. The line commanded by the Earl of Moray was attacked and involved in a fearful fight between ditches and hedges; the earl was killed and his men overcome. Next a band of Englishmen which included ten thousand archers as well as armed men attacked King David, who was ensnared with his men between ditches, and captured by John de Coupland, though not without a substantial fight and the lamentable slaughter of his men. First, however, Coupland had two of his teeth knocked out by a blow from the king, while the king for his part was seriously wounded by two arrows. The tip of one of these could not be extracted by any doctor's skill until the king developed a devotion to St Monan and went there as a pilgrim; while he was standing absorbed in prayer before the saint's statue, the arrow-tip sprang forth a long way as if forcibly pulled out, an event that was not so much a wonder as a miracle. When this happened, the king built the saint's church in noble fashion, as can be seen today, so as not to seem ungrateful for such a benefit; and he endowed it in a kingly manner with very many possessions. As the Scots therefore fled from the two whirlwind attacks so fiercely launched by the English, with the rest of them captured or killed, the Steward of Scotland (that is the king's nephew) and Earl Patrick followed wise advice and saved themselves with the help of an about-turn, so returning home safely. Note how disastrously David, king of Scotland, was defeated and captured along with his army on account of his attack on the lands of the Church of St Cuthbert! Four earls were captured there also along with the king, namely the Earls of Fife, Sutherland, Wigtown and Menteith – this last was later drawn by horses and died after being tortured with various torments. Among the prisoners also were William de Douglas, Walter de Haliburton, and many other nobles, barons, vigorous knights and excellent men-at-arms. Among those killed were John Randolph, earl of Moray, and also the Earl of Stratheam, the Constable of Scotland, the Marischal of Scotland, the Chamberlain of Scotland, the Chancellor of Scotland, David son and heir of Sir David de Lindsay, Roger Cameron, Gilbert de Inchmartine, William Fraser, Andrew Buttergask, John de Boneville and Michael Scot, all knights, along with other barons, knights, men-at-arms and sturdy persons to the number of one thousand men.

(h) Andrew Wyntoun, Orygynale Cronykil of Scotland[28]

When King David passed from home to the Battle of Durham

A thousand and three hundred year
And six and forty thereto clear,
The King of France set him to raise
The siege lying about Calais,
And wrote in Scotland to our king,
And made him right special praying
That he would make war on England;
For, he said, he should take on hand
On his side to make war too;
And so on both the halves they
Should be hard set. Then King David,
That was young, stout and well made,
And yearned for to see fighting,
Agreed to fulfil his yearning,
And gathered his whole host speedily.

He might have been content that he
Already into England thrice

---

[28] From *The Original Chronicle of Andrew of Wyntoun*, ed. F. J. Amours (Scottish Text Society, 1903–14), VI, 168–87. There are three different versions of Wyntoun's *Chronicle*; Amours printed the first and third, and for the second see *Androw of Wyntoun's Orygynale Cronykil of Scotland*, ed. D. Laing (Edinburgh, 1872) (II, 471–7, for the account of Neville's Cross). Amours's first, earliest, version has been followed here; passages which were cut from the later versions are printed in italics, and square brackets are used to denote a passage (at the end of the account) which was added in the later versions. Here, Wyntoun's fifteenth-century Scots has been given modern English spelling, and some words have been translated by Alexander Grant; but Wyntoun's word-order and syntax have been kept unaltered (except for a few paraphrases made in order to preserve the metre or the rhyme). Most of Wyntoun's rhymes still work, but occasionally they have been lost, as for example when the Scots present participle '–and' is modernised to '–ing', or when 'mo' is rendered as 'more'. Despite the 'translation', the flavour, such as it is, of Wyntoun's verse survives. Readers should note his highly ambiguous use of the pronouns 'he', 'him', 'they' and 'them'; in the Latin to which Wyntoun was accustomed, case endings would have prevented ambiguities, and (probably because of that) he seems never to have seen the need to be more specific when he used pronouns in Scots.

Had made war on his enemies.
And all those times he took on hand
To pass again into his land.
Why could he not have been in peace,
And ruled his land in righteousness,
And held himself out of danger?
What stands well, he should not stir.
But since he saw well that Fortune
So fairly with his folk had done,
That through winning in jeopardies
She had raised them in such ways,
That they had won back all his land,
He thought well she would stably stand;
But that is in no kind her law.
Our King Davy could not that know.

Who will of Fortune understand,
Her law is aye to be moving;
False she were, if she should be
Aye standing steadfast in one degree.
Reproved therefore she should not be
For treason or for treachery,
For overturning what is above,
Since Nature makes her so to move,
At times giving great things, at times small,
To make fools to trust that she shall
Aye firmly in that freedom last.
But when they trust her all their best,
All that is given by that lady,
She overturns all suddenly.
What of our folks right so befell,
Without delay I shall you tell.

What was there more? Our King Davy
Gathered his host completely;
And with them of the north country
To Saint Johnstone coming is he.
Ranald of the Isles then,
That was held to be a worthy man,
Came to him out of his country,
With him at that raid to be.
The Earl of Ross was there also,
That to this Ranald was head foe;

157

Therefore he had him there espied,
And within Elcho that nunnery,
Where Ranald had taken lodging then,
He slew him out and his seven men;
And to Ross with his great meinie
Again in haste then turned he.

This Ranald missed was greatly,
He was a good man, and worthy.
And from, they saw, this misfortune,
Some could in their hearts swoon,
And said it was right evil taking,
That at the first of their stirring
That worthy man should be slain so,
And so great crowds desert them now.
And thus amongst them murmured they;
Yet then the king held forth his way,
And for that loss would not abate
To do it that he on was set.

He passed soon the Scottish Sea,
And to the Marches then sped he,
Where at the pele of Liddesdale,
His host to him assembled whole;
Therein was Walter of Selby
Upon the Englishmen's party.
That pele they assailed, and it won,
And all that ever were in it then,
Excepting children and women,
Without mercy they slew then.
They slew them all too cruelly;
Therefore the penalty followed truly.

Then counselled William of Douglas,
That of wars most wise then was,
To turn again to their country:
For they might with their honour high
Return again, he said, right well,
Since they had won by force that pele.
But other great men, that were by,
Said that he had filled fully
His bags, and theirs all empty were;
And said that they might right well fare
To London, for in England then,

Of might there was left no man,
Save cobblers, skinners, or merchants.
For all, they said, were off in France.

The Douglas might not there be heard.
Forth on their way this folk then fared;
And in the Abbey of Hexham
All the host they had there named,
And within all their host they found
Of armed men but two thousand;
And that was all too few of folk to fight
Against of England the great might.

From that abbey they passed then,
As far as Durham in a line,
And in a park well near that town
They lodged them, and took station.

Then had they been in England
Well fourteen days travelling,
But they could get no witting
Of Englishmen's gathering;
The latter they assembled were
Within a park beside them near,
From Trent northwards all the flower
Of folk, that were of any valour.
The Archbishop of York was there,
The Lord Percy, and with them were
The Lord Ferrers, and the Rokeby;
The Lord also de Lucy;
And the Lord Neville yet with them,
Ogle, Heron, and many more men,
That I can not rehearse you here.
Of archers also assembled were,
Twenty thousand, that enrolled were,
Plus men-at-arms, bold as a bear,
That were in all far more than they.
The Scotsmen that in the park lay
Knew nothing of their gathering,
But made them mirth and solacing.

William of Douglas, that then was
Ordained in foraging to pass,
Went out early in the morning
With the most part of their gathering.

Up to the park he held his way
Where that his foes in whole host lay;
And they, that ready were early,
With their battles all suddenly
At the ferry of the hill them met.
Our foragers there hard were set;
And, for they were not of might,
In too great haste they took to flight.
And they eagerly after them,
And so great slaughter of them made,
That both there and at Sundersand,
Five hundred died through blows by hand.
Douglas escaped from the chase.

Our host then all afraid was:
But nonetheless the doughty men
Their host stoutly arrayed then,
And dealt them into battles three:
The king himself in one was he,
And to the Earl John of Moray
And to Douglas too another he gave;
The Steward had the third battle,
That was the greater by a great deal
Than any battle that was there;
For many good men with him were.
And while they arraying were,
The English archers came so near,
That shoot among them well might they.

Then good Sir John the Graham did say
To the King, 'Get me no more
Than a hundred horsed with me to go,
And all yon archers scatter shall I;
So shall we fight more securely.'
Thus spoke he, but he might get none.
His horse in haste then has he taken,
And him alone among them rode,
And rudely room about him made.
When he a-while had pricked there,
And lots of them had made so sore,
He to the battles rode again;
So fell it, that his horse was slain.

The Earl of Moray and his meinie

Was near then to the assembly:
At high dykes assembled they,
And those broke wholly their array.
Therefore discomforted soon were they,
And took their way without delay
To the king, that assembled was
Within a right annoyous place,
Where none, without hurt, might lift a hand,
When they their foes might not withstand.
To the Steward's force then went they,
That was assembled by the way,
Where they had room to stand and fight;
There might they stand to prove their might.
Then both the first forces right there
At that assembly vanquished were.
For of arrows such shooting there was
That lots were wounded in that place.
There was hard fighting; as men says,
Such was never seen before those days,
No harder surely than was there.
For when the fleears two miles and more
Were fled, the banners were still standing,
Face to face still fighting,
With all their force; but nonetheless
Yet were they wholly vanquished.
And many fled, that never again
Returned, and many too were slain.
This fell on Saint Luke's evening
That this battle was struck and given.

There John of Coupland took the king
By force, not yielding in the taking;
The king two teeth out of his head
With a blow of his knife him robbed.
In that fight slain were earls two,
Of Moray and Strathearn were they;
And four were taken to prison,
Of Fife the first, and then Wigtown,
Menteith then, and Sutherland;
These four earls were taken in hand.
Five hundred slain were, as said they,
Plus those that died in the foray:
And so in all that slain were there,

161

To one thousand reckoned were.
Then Sir William of Douglas
Taken in that fighting was;
But the Stewart escaped then,
And with him many of his men,
And the Earl of the March also;
Home to Scotland came those two.
[There taken was the King Davy.
Then was the battle of Crécy:
There was many English men;
The Scots believed therefore then,
That few were left within England
Behind them for to keep the land.]

(i) Extract from the Account Roll of John de Wodehouse
(London, Public Record Office, E 101/25/10)

Item, in wages of 64 men-at-arms,[29] four of them knights, of whom three knights and 42 men-at-arms, 640 mounted archers[30] and 240 foot archers, for five days from 13 October in the twentieth year of the reign, until the seventeenth day of the month inclusive, and one knight, eighteen men-at-arms, and 320 mounted archers for four days within that time, led from Lancashire to the battle near Durham, after they had received wages for eight days from their locality, to set out in the company of the aforesaid archbishop,[31] Henry[32] and Ralph[33] and other magnates in the said war against the Scots the king's enemies, each knight taking 2*s.*, each man-at-arms 1*s.*, each mounted archer 4*d.*, and each foot archer 2*d.*[34] a day, by letters from the said Archbishop of York, Henry and Ralph as appears by a head-count of the said men contained in seven indentures made between John de Leyburn constable in the said war, and John de Wodehouse. £100 13*s.* 4*d.*

Item in wages of 15 men-at-arms leading 29 hobelars[35] and 3,020 mounted archers for four days from 12 October in the said year until the 16th of the month, coming from Yorkshire for the said battle, after their wages for eight days which they had from their locality were used up, each of the said men-at-arms receiving 12*d.*, hobelars 6*d.*, and archers 4*d.* a day, by letters of the said archbishop, Henry and Ralph as appears by a head-count of the said men contained in thirteen indentures made between John de Leyburn, constable, and John de Wodehouse. £207 4*s.* 8*d.*

Item, to John de Haverington, Adam de Hoghton, William de la Legh and Nicholas Botelar, and the men coming with them from the said county of Lancashire for the war, for good equipment, in addition to their wages, by royal gift by means of letters from the said archbishop, Henry and Ralph, £20.

---

[29] A man-at-arms was a fully-equipped cavalryman; he was not necessarily a knight, and would be prepared to fight on foot as well as from horseback.

[30] A mounted archer rode to battle; but fought on foot.

[31] William Zouche, archbishop of York.

[32] Henry Percy.

[33] Ralph Neville.

[34] These are standard wage rates for the period.

[35] A hobelar was a lightly armed horseman.

Illustration 16: Painting of the battle in Paris, BN MS Fr 2643, f. 77v.

A splendid, and wholly inaccurate, fifteenth-century representation of the battle of Neville's Cross from a manuscript of Froissart's Chronicles. The battle is shown taking place outside the walls of Newcastle upon Tyne, in the presence of Queen Philippa. In the left foreground the mounted David II of Scotland is being captured. The armour and equipment shown are those of the fifteenth, not the fourteenth, century, and the fortifications have an inappropriate distinctively French appearance.